GIVERS GAIN
THE BNI STORY

Ivan R. Misner, Ph.D.
with Jeff Morris

Foreword by Don and Nancy Morgan
Canadian National Directors

PARADIGM
PUBLISHING

GIVERS GAIN
The BNI Story

A Paradigm Publishing Book.

To order the book, contact your local bookstore or call 800-688-9394.

ISBN 0-9740819-1-4 hardcover

The authors may be contacted at the following addresses:

Paradigm Publishing
BNI Enterprises Inc.
545 College Commerce Way
Upland, CA 91786-4377
800-825-8286 (outside So. Calif.)
909-608-7575 (in So. Calif.)
909-608-7676 fax

Ivan R. Misner, Ph.D.
misner@bni.com

Jeff Morris
jeff@bookmaestro.com

Credits

Editing: Elisabeth Misner, Bobbie Jo Sims
Proofreading: Deborah Costenbader
Text Design/Production: Jeff Morris
Jacket Design: Jeff Morris, Don Markofski
Index: Linda Webster

First printing: Sept. 2004

To all the members of BNI,
who have made Givers Gain
the world's most successful
organizational principle

CONTENTS

FOREWORD

DON & NANCY MORGAN, CANADIAN FOUNDING NATIONAL DIRECTORS

In March 1995, my first reaction to a BNI chapter was immediate. I knew this program would be a great way to find new contacts and clients. The following week, Nancy visited the chapter and we both sensed that BNI would become valuable to us. We decided to join one of the new BNI chapters where we then lived, in St. Louis Missouri.

Scott Simon, our friend who had just started the St. Louis BNI region, learned that Ivan Misner wanted to expand BNI in other countries and encouraged us to speak with Ivan about taking BNI into Canada.

Things happened pretty quickly. In April, we flew to California for several meetings with Ivan to arrange the purchase of the master franchise for Canada. Ours was the first master franchise that BNI issued, which allowed us to help Ivan smooth out the rough franchise agreement prepared by his lawyers.

During these meetings, Nancy and I came to appreciate Ivan's strong qualities and the completeness of his system for word-of-mouth marketing. Nancy proved prophetic by saying that we should not reinvent the system, but rather learn to work it better than anyone else! We followed the word-of-mouth system Ivan showed us as closely as possible and membership in BNI Canada grew quickly.

We decided starting BNI Canada would work best if we assembled a team of founding Directors to help us. (TEAM = Together Everyone Accomplishes More) It took a little convincing, but we soon arranged for eight Canadian men and women, all very good friends, to make the twenty-hour road trip to St. Louis and tour four BNI Chapters. Of the many side stories to this trip, one is how the Canadians met St. Louis business people and brought them as guests to the St. Louis chapters. It was a funny trip, but at the week's end, Steve and Fran Lawson, Bruce and Eleanor Elliott, and Pam and Jim Sheldon joined Nancy and me to launch BNI Canada.

By June 1, 1995, the master franchise agreement was signed. Nancy and I had been trained in California as the first National Directors and we trained the six founding Canadian Executive Directors. On June 10, 1995, BNI Canada was born. No chapters existed but our team was eager to proceed and just slightly informed. We were a picture of, 'knowledge on ice, but passion on fire'.

Just before starting our first chapters, the entire team drove to New York to attend a BNI Director's Conference. There were about thirty folks, which included the Canadians. We mention this as a comparison to the BNI Director conference nine years later, attended by more than three hundred Directors from five continents. Since 1995, the entire BNI organization has grown significantly and truly deserves the slogan, "The" Business Referral Organization.

Get Ready. Get Set. Go

Like so many new BNI members, we didn't know the best way to invite people to BNI. Of course there were no chapters for people to observe.

Each team started differently. The Lawsons spoke with their past business associates. The Sheldons relied on their rich contact group who helped refer potential members. Bruce Elliott's natural gregarious personality allowed him to strike up conversations anywhere, even in grocery checkout lines. One popular BNI audio is Bruce Elliott speaking about how, "Inviting Can Be Easy". Nancy and I were to start chapters in downtown Toronto where we had no business contacts. We employed the chilly process of cold calling people with interesting newspaper ads. We also walked into neighborhood shops and we even forced ourselves to talk to people in the streets. Our technique was to recite a sales script we pasted together from early BNI promotional materials.

Our first information session was scheduled in a fancy hotel meeting room for 7 AM. We got ready at 6:15 AM. By 6:45 we were set to begin. We became very nervous at 7:05 AM when not one of the 15 people we invited showed up. After what seemed like hours, (but was minutes) the first person arrived and soon nine people were eating our Danish pastries and hearing our first BNI presentation. Our first downtown chapter started nine weeks later, giving tangible evidence that the system worked.

We experienced first hand the power of business networking employed as a tool to start businesses. By following the proven BNI networking system, we developed forty-four chapters in our first year. A universal truth about business became apparent. All businesses need new customers and clients and prefer to have referred clients land in their laps. This sparked Bruce Elliott to create our first memory hook, "Don't skip breakfast, it could be hazardous to your wealth".

A Little Training Goes A Long Way

In August 1996, Ivan Misner came to Toronto to give us a few pointers. His comments made us realize that we still had a lot to learn about referral marketing. Steve Lawson, thinking about the result of forty-four new chapters in our first year piped up, "Well, if we've been all wrong, imagine what will happen when we start to get it right!"

With renewed confidence that BNI would work throughout Canada, we fine-tuned our goals and set an objective to have chapters networked 7,800 kilometers across Canada.

Soon, Bill Becks joined the team to set up the region surrounding Barrie, Ontario and chapters spread throughout Ontario. By the third year, we were close to our objective with chapters in Halifax, on the Atlantic and Victoria on the Pacific Ocean.

Doing business across Canada presents special challenges because of the vast distances and a dual language requirement. Finding translators 'native' to Quebec, we translated the major BNI manuals and forms into French. Nancy kicked off the first Montreal chapter in December 1997, and followed with ten more chapters. She then focused on recruiting a strong bi-lingual team who were passionate about BNI. We now understood the important role played by BNI Directors and Ambassadors in the success of a BNI chapter. To get great results, BNI staff and the chapter Leadership Group must work as a single focused management team.

There are many interesting Canadian stories. One story comes from the Montreal WIT chapter, which with seventy-eighty members is currently the largest in the world. This chapter admired the BNI structure but also wanted to maintain their autonomy. Fortunately, a few strong members understood the importance of 'sticking to the system' and heeded our advice about building a strong foundation for their chapter. The WIT chapter consistently has a very strong leadership executive group, a powerful membership committee and ensures that all other chapter leadership positions are filled with well-trained members. Generating more than five hundred referrals per month, the chapter demonstrates the power of experienced people complying with the demands of a structured program.

Ours is an interesting case study as we quickly evolved from a 'mom and pop' venture to a boutique-marketing agency. It wasn't long before our business advisors suggested planning for two national BNI offices located in Toronto and Vancouver to better serve eastern and western Canada. This objective was finally achieved during the summer of 2003.

Gateway To The World: A New Business Paradigm

By 1998, Executive Director Steve Lawson, had helped his brother start BNI UK, another team, Pam and Jim Sheldon started BNI Australia, and yet another started BNI Maryland and BNI Chicago.

Along with being instrumental in opening other BNI host nations, we started more than two hundred Canadian chapters in our first five years. This expansion, and Canada's huge geographic territory, stretched our administrative and staffing resources beyond their limits. We learned a lesson about businesses imploding from explosive growth.

Slowing our membership growth allowed us to begin building a more comprehensive administrative structure to support the growing Canadian organization. This meant mastering new technologies, hiring and training new staff, and designing new marketing resources. We invested in our growth by hiring Christel Wintels as our marketing Director. Christel came to our attention as an effective Chapter President where she also represented her marketing agency. We slowly began to discover and understand the use of specific promotional resources that are most effective for our unique word-of-mouth program.

Technological advances also influenced us. Our stand-alone computers were soon replaced by small network systems. We explored how best to use websites, flash presentations and one of our Directors, Jim Sheldon, developed software to digitize our out-dated paper and pencil member database. His initial work became the forerunner of our current BNINET global intranet system that now controls the BNI member database. Training directed toward the membership and chapter leadership has always been a large component of the BNI program. With more than seventy full and part-time BNI staff stretched coast-to-coast, programs for staff training are becoming equally important.

From our Personal growth experiences; we discovered how to manage explosive growth from referred business. At times, it is useful to shift gears and modify one's request for referrals. When business begins to crush your existing resources, don't quit the BNI chapter but instead ask for referral of advisors who can help you restructure your business to handle an increased client base.

Change and Adaptation From Learning

BNI is not a static organization. New ideas coming from thousands of talented BNI Directors and members often show up as new marketing strategies and techniques. Some programs prove to be universally beneficial in helping members increase their referred business. Notable examples are the, BNI Chapter Mentoring, MSP and Power Team programs. The genesis of these programs are traced back to early work developed by Bill Becks, Christel Wintels and the many Canadian Directors, Ambassadors and members who helped test and evolve these important systems.

Many Directors and members became contributing authors to, Masters of Networking and Masters of Success. These best selling books provide high-achieving members further clues to obtaining success in their lives and businesses. The phrase, "turning contacts into contracts", is a direct spin-off from these works. The books also inspired Mary Anne Marriott to create the first community "Network Organization Trade Show" in Halifax. The "Networking Month" in Australia and networking award Galas for BNI members throughout Canada and the world, were also created from these books.

BNI works best for high achievers. These members demand that we continue testing and improving the BNI marketing system. Our goal is to sustain a revolution of rising expectations between BNI members and staff. We want members to master new strategies and techniques in referral marketing, because these successes fuel the research and development of yet newer referral strategies and techniques.

A Great Way To Get Business and Better Way to Do Business

At times, it seems like we are just getting started. Yet, we know the combined efforts of BNI members and BNI staff, are making an impact on the way business is conducted in Canada. Canadian BNI members generate thousands of referrals monthly, resulting in tens of millions of dollars in new referred business. Large Canadian businesses are noticing the BNI brand and encouraging their employees to join a local BNI chapter. Our first organizational objective created a referral-marketing program networked across Canada. Our next large organizational objective is to provide dynamic and inspired leadership in referral marketing to help guide dedicated members to higher levels of business performance.

Our future approaches rapidly. BNI Canada, and other BNI host nations, will continue to experience an increased number of chapters and more members per chapter. Our 'Power of Forty' program is challenging more chapters to grow to thirty-forty members. As we influence a larger portion of the Canadian labor force, more people are coming to understand that BNI is a, "great way to get more business and a better way to do business".

When we started in the mid 1990s, some people described BNI and word-of-mouth marketing as a 'cult'. Now, ten years later, word-of-mouth marketing is a buzzword in the marketing industry and BNI is still leading this 'best kept marketing secret, word-of-mouth marketing'.

We anticipate arriving at a time when a significant percentage of the employed Canadian population know that, "BNI is the only serious choice for business referrals" and then ask, "How can I get in?"

chapter 1

FIRST THINGS FIRST
WHY I WROTE THIS BOOK

I ALREADY KNOW WHY YOU'RE HOLDING THIS BOOK IN YOUR HANDS. IT'S because you've become a member of an organization that you feel pretty good about — an organization that has grown from one chapter to thousands since 1985 because it has earned a reputation as a potent referral generator for business people around the world.

I also know that not too many people can tell you how this came to pass. It's true that many of BNI's current members and leaders have been here a long time, some even from the beginning. They can tell you their own personal history in the organization, because many of them were the first BNI members and leaders in their part of the country or the world.

But none of them can tell you, from a single viewpoint, exactly how it all began and how it got to be the organization you see today. That task uniquely falls to the Founder. And it's not really a task, because I enjoy telling stories. Many of my friends and colleagues will attest to that, and usually they're polite about it.

More and more over the last few years, I've become aware that it's not only a story that I'd like to tell, but one that *needs* to be told.

Until now, nobody has written down the whole story, or even tried to tell it in more than generalizations and anecdotes. Truth be told, telling the full story out loud would require an audience equipped with monklike stoicism and flanks of iron. That's why books were invented.

In the pages that follow, I'll try to recount for you, as succinctly and vividly as I can, how BNI sprang into existence and how it became so large and successful in such a short time. This won't be the whole story by a long shot — but I hope it's enough to give you the picture, the sense, and the flavor of the fine organization you belong to.

One of the secrets of our success is that BNI is made up of a lot of people who bring talent, skill, and dedication to the job. BNI is not built on me, or on the National Directors and me, or even on just the National/Executive/Regional/Area/Assistant Directors and me. It's built on all of us — hundreds of directors, thousands of Leadership Teams, and tens of thousands of BNI members, not to mention a lot of support people.

And yet — if you add up all these people and their time and dedication, it still doesn't account for the phenomenon that BNI has become.

It's a familiar mystery. BNI is a classic example of the whole being greater than the sum of its individual parts. Every one of us adds something good and positive and significant to the organization, but when the recipe is put together and cooked in a unique way, the result is far beyond anything you might expect. BNI has taken on a life of its own, creating results in surprising ways and in surprising places.

I think one reason BNI is so much greater than the sum of its parts is because the parts are encouraged — more than encouraged, they're trained and exhorted — to interact with one another. The key to the effectiveness of networking is forming relationships based on trust in an atmosphere of generosity and selflessness. This is the key to BNI's organizational health, as well. The only competition among members is a friendly scramble to see who can do the most good for others. That's constructive competition.

What's behind this generous organizational spirit? It's a philosophy that's expressed in the title of this book. This philosophy sets us apart from other organizations and enables us to build a company that is uniquely positive. It is an organizational culture unlike any other in the world, a culture that can be expressed in two words that are foremost in the mind of every member: **Givers Gain.**

Inspiration shows itself everywhere, and it too is shared. Our directors are among the most skilled and innovative organization leaders in the world, and they are not shy about expressing their opinions on how BNI could be made more effective and its members more productive.

In an organization composed top to bottom of business leaders, no one has a corner on the idea market. I would estimate that three-quarters of the most useful ideas occur to a director, or to me personally, after one of us sees something new being tried in a chapter meeting that might work well in all the other chapters. I get a lot of satisfaction watching this great assemblage of minds create its own "Eureka!" moments, over and over again.

This collective creativity is awe-inspiring — and unlike many other organizations, BNI has a central philosophy that encourages the sharing of good ideas. People say to each other, "Hey, this has worked well for me — you should try it!"

Aside from the unpredictable synergy of philosophy and function that characterizes BNI, there are other factors in its phenomenal growth — factors that are common knowledge and certainly no secret to successful people. One of them is the art of making decisions.

Someone I respect once said to me, "Look, Ivan, not every decision you make has to be right. You just have to make more right decisions than wrong ones. And when you realize you've made a wrong decision, you've got to fix it quick."

This is a wonderfully comforting thing to hear, especially for a person who never expected to end up running a worldwide organization with a life and a mind of its own. What if we take a wrong turn? Will we suddenly find ourselves on the rocks?

I've made my share of wrong decisions, but I've learned to correct them quickly. On the whole, my advisors and I have made a lot more right decisions than wrong ones. The essential thing is to make decisions. Deciding not to decide is always the wrong decision.

Another factor is the quality of the people who are attracted to BNI. Because the up-front philosophy of BNI makes receiving secondary to giving, you won't run across many selfish or self-absorbed people. You'll find very few members who are pessimists, naysayers, or dyed-in-the-wool cynics. The negative types tend to weed themselves out. It's tough to commit to something you're not wired to believe in.

What you will find is members and leaders who are wholeheartedly positive about life and generous toward others. If they get down in the dumps about anything, it's about not having enough time to do everything they want to do for their families, their businesses, their fellow BNI members, and anyone else who crosses their path. Their altruism is rather daunting; among people who are naturally competitive, the competition becomes who's tops in doing things for others.

What you read in the pages that follow will be a quick history of BNI from the first glimmer of inspiration to its full flowering as a global organization. But I don't want this to be a dull recitation of names and dates, or a geography lesson, or a collection of charts and graphs, as impressive as any of those pieces might be on its own. Instead, I want to show you the thinking — by me and by others — that went on behind all the big decisions and actions. At heart this is a fully human story — not just my story, but the stories of scores of other thinkers and leaders and business owners who are the driving force behind our success.

For that reason, I'm going to reminisce a bit. I'll tell you what we were thinking and when, who was involved, what we decided and why, what we ended up doing, and what we learned along the way. Like Uncle Ed on the front porch, I'll tell you some stories that are slightly shaggy but that you may find entertaining or educational — or even both.

In a later chapter I'll sum it all up by telling you about the things we consider to be BNI's traditions. Some of these — most of them, probably — you will have gathered from the pages of BNI history that follow and the personal anecdotes embedded in them. In that chapter you'll get a better picture of how these traditions work together to make BNI not only a powerful business tool but a uniquely effective force for good.

Most of all, I hope that when you finish reading this book, you'll have a bird's-eye perspective of BNI to go with your experience of its day-to-day, week-by-week functioning at the chapter level. You already know that you've joined the world's most successful referral networking organization. You probably have your own stories to tell about the good it's done for your business. Now you will know how it got that way.

So . . . pull up a rocker, get comfortable, and let the story begin.

chapter 2

THE FIRST CHAPTER
1984–1985

"WHEN YOU STARTED BNI BACK IN 1985, DID YOU EVER THINK IT WOULD get this big?" That's a question I seem to get asked a lot these days.

Well, as I often tell people, it's good to have goals. But I can't honestly say it was my goal back then to create an organization with tens of thousands of members passing billions of dollars worth of referrals in thousands of chapters in dozens of countries on several continents. Nor did I have any idea such a thing could happen so fast.

When I started that first chapter, I wasn't even thinking of BNI as a business. I already had my own company; I just needed a way to round up more business for it.

But somewhere along the way, I got sidetracked. Funny how things sometimes work out, isn't it?

STARTING UP

Let me back up a bit and get a running start. I was born in Pittsburgh and raised in Southern California, with a strong family background that included terrific parents. With help from them, a couple of scholarships, and some student loans, I worked my way through college and earned a Ph.D. from the University of Southern California. After a brief stint in the US Department of Commerce, I decided that private business was where the future was.

Before long I was not only a partner in a trucking company, I also worked part time in my own company, AIM Consulting, in La Verne,

California, about 25 miles east of downtown Los Angeles. With my academic background in organizational behavior and development, I specialized in helping other companies hire, train, and evaluate employees and create personnel policies and procedure manuals. I also guided marketing departments, especially in the growing retail computer field, in hiring and training people before they brought in permanent managers.

By early 1984, things were changing. I was consulting full time. Business was good enough to let me invest in a new house, but no sooner had I moved in than I learned I was losing my biggest client, whose business, unbeknownst to me, was in the process of failing.

Banks are funny about home mortgage loans. Mine felt I should pay every month. I had to bring in more business, and fast. What was the best way to do that?

I looked at my options. Advertising? It's a necessity for many businesses, especially retail, and it can be very effective — but my market was limited and hard to target. A barely adequate ad campaign would cost a lot more than I could afford.

I tried direct mail. The experts say a 2 percent response is considered good in a direct mail effort. As a business consultant, I got zero.

I could put together a massive public relations program, but as a consultant, my costs and limitations were a lot like those of advertising.

I could lock myself in my office with a coffee pot and a telephone and start cold-calling people to ask for their business. I knew how to cold-call. I had trained whole marketing departments on how to do it. In fact, I worked with them so long that I knew I never wanted to do another cold call — ever again. There had to be a better way.

Actually, the answer was fairly obvious to me. I was already getting most of my new business from referrals and from speaking engagements. I knew that my highest-quality, longest-lasting, best-paying clients were those who had been referred to me by other clients. So I began contacting my remaining clients to get referrals.

Then I started thinking. Of all the kinds of business that came to me, the best business came in by referral — yet I had no reliable way of increasing the number of referrals I received. Like most business people, I got referrals through an informal network of business acquaintances, but mostly as an afterthought. If the opportunity arose, and if the thought occurred, one business person might say to a client or acquaintance, "You ought to go see So-and-So — he can get that done for you." Then he might or might not call to let you know he had sent that person to see you.

What we needed was a networking system designed from the ground up to do a single thing well: generate the largest possible number of high-quality referrals for all members, from as many different sources as possible, for the mutual benefit of all — members, customers, vendors, friends, and everyone else — and to do it in a positive way.

I felt there was a huge, untapped potential for creating and sharing referrals among business people like me. Was there a systematic way to tap this potential? In the closing months of 1984, that became my challenge.

REFERRALS, PLEASE

I was already getting occasional referrals by participating in a variety of networking organizations in my area — service groups, for example. Their primary purpose is to provide service to the community, and that's the reason you join, although many will tell you that service groups are also a good way to make business contacts. As an active member, you naturally meet a lot of important people and form relationships. But these relationships don't necessarily lead to business referrals very quickly. In some service groups, you end up competing with fellow members for referrals.

I was a member of the local chamber of commerce. That was a good place to meet other business people, especially the movers and shakers, but it became obvious to me that unless you sat on committees, attended mixers regularly, met with the officers, or volunteered to greet visitors and members, the contacts tended to be rather casual, not focused on giving or receiving business referrals.

Because my partner in AIM Consulting was a woman, I joined two women's networking groups that were strong on education and had a clear and coherent vision. One was a nationwide knowledge networking group, the other a business referral group. Knowledge networking is important in business and professional development, but

I was a member of the chamber of commerce for Arcadia. I used to go through the cards to see the new members coming in, and those were potential leads. So I would write them a letter telling them I'd like them to join us at breakfast . . . and I got to meet all the business people in the community.
—Lee Shimmin, insurance agent
Founding member of BNI

the national group was more suitable for women than for men, and it didn't focus on referrals. The other group, a local women's referral group, was not particularly effective in fulfilling its nominal purpose. However, I did get a number of referrals — because, as one of the few men in a women's group, I stuck in people's memory.

Some of the organizations I've mentioned are what is known as "casual contact" networks. These are somewhat haphazard in their approach to generating good, productive, long-lasting, referral-generating business contacts. I also joined a strong-contact group, whose members were dedicated to getting and giving referrals. Unfortunately, this particular group treated its members like junior high students, penalizing trivial missteps and oversights. Over time, its leadership tended to drift off the organization's procedures and mission. Nobody had a good time in this group; if you were one minute late, you were fined. If you forgot to hand somebody your card, you were fined. If it was a full moon on a Tuesday, you were fined.

I felt that each of the groups I joined had different things to offer in terms of personal relationships, business development, referrals, service to the community, contact with people in different fields of interest, frequent regular meetings, consistency, and discipline. However, no single group satisfied all my requirements. None embodied the main thing I was looking for, which was a system of mutually beneficial networking based on business referrals in a positive environment.

New Ideas

Finally, in frustration, I approached several business people I knew and trusted, and who knew and trusted me, who were in these groups. I asked them if they would be interested in forming a new type of group — a focused, positive organization that would be structured and operated entirely to promote networking.

I told them some of the things I had been thinking about.

I wanted our group to be built around the idea of mutual benefit, the concept that our first duty would be to help others in the group get high-quality business referrals and to help them in any other way that we could. The breadth and depth of such a network would automatically end up helping us as much as everyone else.

I wanted the meetings to be command performances, with every member required to attend every week without fail, so the network would stay close-knit and strong.

I wanted to take the best features of the many different networks I was involved in and create a single, powerful group. I also wanted us to play around with new ideas, to find a formula that would bring in plenty of lucrative business referrals for everybody, to change things to see what would happen, and to stick with whatever we found worked best.

I wanted us to enjoy ourselves while we were doing it, to look on it not only as a business function but also as a network of personal relationships, like an extended family.

Three of my networking acquaintances jumped on the idea. Yes, they would be glad to meet and talk about forming a new kind of network. They would call their friends and invite them to join us and contribute their own ideas. They agreed with me that there must be a better way to market their businesses and interact with other professionals.

That's how we came together at our first meeting, in Arcadia, California, December 1984. Joining me were Carolyn Denny, a CPA; Lee Shimmin, an insurance agent; and Mike Ryan, a financial planner — all of whom are still involved in BNI today.

THE NETWORK

We didn't get going officially that December; instead, we decided to hold our first formal meeting the following month, January 1985. I didn't live that close to Arcadia, but most of my interested colleagues did, so we chose to meet there. We spent most of our December get-together talking about our goals and how to run the meetings to achieve them. We also decided to give ourselves a simple, descriptive name: The Network. (From here on out, though, I'm going to use the name we decided on a few years later, the name we all now know and love: BNI.)

I offered at least one of my fellow organizers a partnership in the enterprise, but I got no takers. No problem, I thought. How much trouble would it be to keep one chapter going? A few phone calls each week, maybe a small amount of paperwork. The Leadership Team — President, Vice President, and Secretary/Treasurer — would keep things humming along nicely. After all, this was not my business. I was a consultant; the group was just a tool to help my friends and me bring in more business.

AN AIM CONSULTING AFFILIATE

Here's the way it would work, we decided: First, to avoid competition within the chapter, only one member per professional category would be allowed to join. We would show up once a week at breakfast — same day, same place every week — without fail. Because every member had business commitments that could not and should not be ignored, we would follow a strict agenda and would begin and end each meeting on time.

I sat down at my typewriter one evening and typed up an agenda that I thought would be a good way to conduct the weekly meeting. It would help us get to know each other, learn about each other's businesses, and bring in referrals for everyone. This single sheet of paper became our starting point. Although we would make a number of changes and refinements over the years, the Agenda would serve as the backbone for all future BNI chapter meetings. It contained the essentials for creating and maintaining an effective referral network.

We would spend the first part of the meeting standing up by turns and giving a 60-second "commercial" describing our products or services. We would introduce guests and visitors.

Next, in weekly rotation, one of us would give a 10- to 15-minute presentation on a topic related in some way to our business. This talk might be on the history of our industry, useful advice or guidance, news about coming advances in technology, or even a product demonstration.

This is an important part of my personal success, my professional success, which really does tie to the early skills I learned, because as you practice different things with a group of people, you start to learn what works and what doesn't.

—Carolyn Denny, CPA
Founding member of BNI

Then would come the central element of the meeting, our reason for being. After the main presentation, members would pass referrals to other members, telling them about a prospect they had had contact with who might need their products or services and who had been told to expect a call, a letter, or a visit from the business person the member had recommended. After that was done, the meeting would adjourn and we would go to work.

We felt this approach would be the most efficient and effective way to generate referrals week after week. It would be very structured, very organized, very goal-oriented.

It was all about commitment. You paid money to join, because you knew that, if you followed the system, you would get it back many times over in new business. You would show up as promised and, if at all possible, you would have at least one referral for a fellow member.

GOOD VIBES

One thing we vigorously agreed on was that we would maintain a positive, constructive atmosphere. No fines. No petty rules about shaking hands. No "casual contact" networking. No gender-based limitations. Yes, structure and rules were crucial, but our members would be treated as responsible adults. Have to miss a meeting? Fine, just send someone to stand in for you, represent your business, and give and receive referrals for you.

Although we wanted to make it as positive as possible, we also understood, early on, that we had to use "tough love." Balance was the key; there had to be rules, but enforcement had to be positive in nature. We had to have systems of accountability to keep our chapters from turning into coffee klatches or social clubs.

Problems with a member's behavior? We designed a Membership Committee whose function would be to solve problems that kept a person from being a valuable, productive member. The approach would be constructive: "What can we do to help you to show up at meetings regularly?" or "How can we help you solve this quality problem that's keeping our members from recommending you to others?"

Only as a last resort would a member be asked to leave the group. And even this would be presented in positive terms: the member would be informed that the chapter would open his classification, so that a new person in that profession could apply for membership. It was as simple and direct as that.

FIRST KICKOFF

We held the first official meeting of BNI in January 1985 in Arcadia. Those of us who attended the December meeting had invited others to come check us out, and to become charter members if they liked the concept. As a result, we had 20 people at our first official meeting. This was encouraging. Even more amazing and encouraging, most of our visitors decided to join that very day. It seemed we had hit upon a magic formula.

It wasn't all work. We were becoming close friends and learning to trust each other. Trust is one of the most important aspects of a good networking relationship, and we were careful to build trust in every way possible — in doing business, in helping each other solve problems, and in forming, in many cases, lifelong friendships. To this day, I continue to do business with Carolyn, Lee, and Mike, and I count them among my closest and most enduring friends and associates.

It didn't escape my notice that many of us who formed the first core group were in professions that worked together symbiotically and were naturally inclined to refer business to one another. Insurance agents and accountants, for example, did not compete with each other but could, in different ways, help clients manage their finances. These professions, like many others, also depended heavily on referrals for new business. The connections between other professionals, such as chiropractors and interior decorators, were less pronounced, but still rich with potential for referrals. **Although the concept didn't come into clear focus in my mind until later, this was our first example of two important BNI networking concepts, Contact Spheres, and later, Power Partners.** A Contact Sphere is all the possible professions a networker can team up with; Power Partners are all the people the networker has actually teamed up with.

I knew that we already had the beginnings of a lively, growing, productive group of networkers representing many professions and specialties, passing referrals by the handful and eager to help one another's business take off. What I didn't quite realize, however, was how fast this new organization would grow. Like Jack's magic beanstalk, BNI was about to shoot toward the sky.

Yes, it does work. I don't do any advertising, I don't do any mailers, I don't do seminars, but I still get somewhere between 60 and 70 referrals a year.

—Mike Ryan, financial advisor Founding member of BNI

chapter 3

THE FIRST YEAR
1985

WITHIN A FEW WEEKS AFTER OUR FIRST MEETING, WE HAD GAINED SO MANY
new members that we outgrew our first restaurant and had to find
another, and not long after that, still another. This was inconvenient,
but all in all, a positive sign of success.

In March, however, we came up against another wall. A woman
who visited our group was immediately eager to join. "This is great!"
she said. "It's really organized. I love this! I can get a ton of business
out it! But I can't join this group because you already have a member
who does what I do" — which was using a computer to compose news-
letters, a fairly new and uncommon specialty.

She came to me with a request: "Will you help me open another
chapter?"

I thought, Sure, why not? Two chapters, plus my consulting
practice, I can handle that. So we started another chapter, this time in
Pasadena. She brought a couple of dozen people to that meeting, most
of them duplicating the professions we had already covered in our first
group, but with some new professions represented as well. We enlisted
our first dentist in this chapter — Dr. Jim LaBriola, who is one of
BNI's longest-lasting members and sponsor of innumerable referrals
over the years.

At the Kickoff of this second group, I gave a talk to the new members, telling them what BNI was all about. I invited visitors to join, which
they scrambled to do, because we emphasized that those first to apply
would get favored consideration, and that second place was no place.

Well, it turned out that two of the people at that Kickoff were beat out by their competitors who had jumped at the chance to sign up. They came up to me at the end of the meeting and said, "Wow, this is a great idea! I could get a lot of business out of a group like this! If you'll help each of us start our own chapters, you can run four of these."

And I thought, Okay, four chapters and my consulting business. I can do that.

So we opened up two more, one in West Los Angeles and one in Diamond Bar. The same thing happened at those Kickoffs. Dozens more joined BNI. People in both groups wanted to start new chapters. Before long I found myself thinking, Okay, eight chapters and my consulting practice. I can handle that.

I did not suspect until months later just how fast this idea would catch on and how quickly new chapters would be formed. By the end of the first year, we had opened 20 chapters across Southern California.

Twenty chapters and my consulting business. I can handle that. I think.

GROWING WILD

Sometime in that first year, it began to dawn on me that my idea had struck a chord. I knew that getting referrals was important to me as a consultant, but I hadn't realized just how important it was to all business people — that all business people had this hunger for an organized networking system with a positive approach.

Especially a networking system that would stay focused on getting referrals. There were a lot of networking groups out there already, but as everybody in them became good friends, most groups seemed to turn into coffee klatches.

One of the strengths of a networking organization is that everybody becomes friends — and one of the weaknesses of a networking organization is that everybody becomes friends. The strength becomes a weakness because people don't always hold friends accountable. Keeping everybody's eye on the ball, keeping a chapter focused on giving and getting referrals, requires holding friends accountable.

Turning into a coffee klatch was only one of the dangers BNI faced as it grew. Growth naturally brings change, and distance brings change. BNI was growing in both numbers and reach. I stayed pretty busy traveling from chapter to chapter, kicking off new groups and welcoming new members, and revisiting chapters as they matured and expanded.

Toward the end of our first year, I could see that one of our weaknesses was keeping the chapters working off the same script. I would visit chapter X five months after Kickoff and find that they had stopped having members give their 10-minute presentations. In chapter Y, 10 months along, members were skipping breakfast so they could meet later or sneak out early.

Many of us in the founding group knew, from experience with other organizations, that certain basic meeting elements would work for us and others would not. It was important that all chapters follow a system that was known to consistently work. Otherwise, visitors to drifting chapters would soon begin to conclude that BNI didn't work as advertised, and that would be the beginning of the end. BNI would go the way of so many other groups.

Catching the Train

Toward the end of the year, I attended a meeting of one chapter where the only way I knew I was at a BNI meeting was that everyone was wearing a badge that said BNI. They didn't follow the Agenda at all, and it had turned into a coffee klatch. This started some alarm bells ringing in my mind.

Not long afterward, I visited another BNI chapter where everything seemed normal until, to my great surprise, the meeting ended without a certain vital element having taken place. "Oh, you mean the referral part?" said the President. "You know what, we stopped doing that at the meeting. It was too embarrassing. We were putting people on the spot. Now we do referrals after the meeting. It's all right, the Vice President still gets a copy."

"And how's that working for you?" I said, in my best Dr. Phil manner.

"Well, I don't know. I haven't seen the VP's report."

We got together with the VP. It immediately became apparent that their referrals had fallen by half since they had stopped passing them in the meeting. This gave me a chance to use one of my favorite expressions.

"Based on results," I said, "do you think this is working?"

To their credit, they admitted that it wasn't. They had learned an important lesson: accountability is critical.

Both these experiences taught me an important lesson, too. Seeing how quickly our grand design could get watered down or lost made me realize that this was a challenge that had to be met head-on. And we already had the tools in hand — our training program.

To me, training has been an important element of BNI from the beginning. Our reason for existing is to help each other get referrals and to tell each other about our products and services. Many business people, particularly the owners of small businesses, have no idea how to network effectively. Others may know the principles but not be up to snuff in their presentation skills. BNI helps members refine their presentation skills and marketing approaches. For many small businesses, too small to have their own marketing department, our group is the only effective form of marketing they will use, or can use.

In developing BNI from the ground level, I felt that part of this networking training would happen as a matter of course because of the way we had designed our meeting Agenda. If members had to stand and deliver at every meeting, they would gradually lose their stage fright and become more confident presenters. They were limited to 60 seconds, so they had to think carefully about what was important to say regarding their business, versus what was not important or not interesting. We would offer additional training in these matters as part of the membership package.

We also felt it was important to train our leadership. In the beginning, we did this chapter by chapter. There was core-group training to help the chapter organizers bring in the members needed to form a working chapter. There was Leadership Team training to help the chapter officers run their groups effectively. As we expanded across Southern California, we found it necessary to divide up into regions, so we hired and trained Regional Directors to coordinate between chapters and the main office and to conduct leadership training at the regional level.

The opportunity to give a 60-second commercial at weekly meetings forced me to do two things I had never done before: evaluate my business, and talk about it in front of others.

—Linda Macedonio
Co-Executive Director
BNI Rhode Island & Cape Cod

I worked to come up with new and better ways of training the Leadership Team — President, Vice President, and Secretary/Treasurer — and more effective ways of conducting our meetings. The result was the birth of one of our most powerful tools, the *BNI Directors' Manual.*

Training was a way of maintaining an efficient, yet responsive, networking organization. We didn't want BNI to develop a permanent hierarchy, run by career bosses, with no voice for its members; instead, we wanted everybody to participate. We would encourage all members to realize their full potential and to understand that leadership was theirs if they wanted it and trained for it. Chapters would elect new officers every six months.

Many of the skills that good marketers use to sell themselves and their products or services are the same skills that leaders use to unite a networking group, accomplish its objectives, and fulfill its mission. Training new leaders every six months, as well as retraining leaders and members at regular intervals, could only enhance their marketing and networking skills and strengthen the group as a functioning entity.

Simply being great at what you do is not enough. To make a business successful, you must relinquish some of the technical and managerial work and become a marketer as well.

—Patti Salvucci
Executive Director
BNI Boston

INNOVATION AND TRADITION

Although we were very focused on training to keep our operations consistent and uniform, we were alert to the need for organizational growth and learning. We made a lot of changes as we grew, because in those exciting early years we were learning quickly what worked and what didn't. We made many mistakes, and as soon as we saw they were mistakes, we set about correcting them. We tried and discarded many ideas that we thought were brilliant, and we incorporated some simple, no-brainer ideas that turned out to be immensely valuable. I was emphatic about getting the suggestions and opinions of members and leaders everywhere as to how we could make BNI more effective in performing its central function, generating referrals.

Once we learned what worked, we were determined to keep it going, to make sure it was quickly adopted across the whole organization and passed along to new chapters as they arose. In other words, it was turned into a BNI tradition.

Here's a good example of how we did this. When we were still in our one-chapter stage, we were already following a meeting Agenda very much like what we use today. The basics were all there. First, we stood up in turn and gave our 60-second commercials. Then we introduced our visitors. Next, our main speaker. After that, we passed referrals.

During this last part, if you had a referral to pass, you stood up when your turn came and said, "I have two referrals for Joe and one for Angela, and here's what they are." If you didn't have any referrals, you simply said, "Pass," and the next person would take her turn.

We'd been meeting about two months, and at the end of one meeting the chiropractor in our group came to me and said, "Ivan, I haven't gotten a single referral yet. Now, I know it takes time, but here's what concerns me: nobody has even come up to talk to me or ask a question about chiropractic care. When I go somewhere and run into people I know, they'll usually talk about chiropractic, but nobody knows me here, and they stay away from the subject. It makes me think nobody in this room has ever been to a chiropractor. If that's the case, how can they refer me?"

I said, "You're right. You've got to get them to use you so they can refer you. Why don't you offer a free initial consultation to get them to come in and see what you do and how it works? Then they'll be able to refer you.

"Here's what you can do. At next week's meeting, just stand up and tell everybody that you'll do a free first visit, even throw in an X-ray, and do an adjustment, so they can see what chiropractic care is all about."

We had a couple of dozen members. Know how many took him up on his offer? One. One guy said he'd go visit the chiropractor.

The chiropractor came up to me at the end of the meeting and said, "Brilliant idea, Ivan. They didn't exactly flock to me."

I said, "No, they didn't, did they? I'm really sorry about that, but keep it up. It's a start. You had zero, now you've got one. See how it goes. It may take some time."

The following week, the meeting was moving along nicely, we were passing referrals, and it came around to this guy who had gone to the chiropractor after the last meeting. He stood up, hesitated, looked at me, and said, "Ivan, I don't have a referral today, but I don't want to pass."

Now, to understand why he hesitated, you need to know what kind of guy I am. I like for things to move along quickly, efficiently, on time and on schedule, don't get sidetracked, snap snap snap. I wasn't the founder of a networking organization just dropping in to visit; I was the President of the chapter, following the Agenda, getting us through the meeting in the most efficient way possible. I had written the Agenda for efficiency, in my own style, and members were already accustomed to the drill: stand up and give your referrals, or if you don't have one, just say, "Pass," and let the next person have his turn. Snap snap snap.

So this guy was saying, "I don't want to pass." I hesitated.

I said, " . . . O-o-o-kay, then, uh . . . what do you want to do?"

He said, "Well, I'd like to say a few words."

I said, "O-o-o-kay, well, uh, what do you want to say?"

He said, "Well, I just want to talk about Dr. Rubin. I went to see him last week, and I went in and got this X-ray, and he showed me all around his facility, explained all the things that he did, and then he did an adjustment.

"Now, I've had this lower back pain for about seven years," he said. "Nothing incapacitating, just a nagging ache that if I stand up too long it starts bothering me.

"I've gotta tell you," he said, "for the first time in seven years, my back doesn't hurt! You're all crazy if you don't take him up on this offer!

"I just wanted to say that," he said, and sat down.

I looked around the room and saw all these people picking up pens and filling out referral slips for the chiropractor, and I thought, Omigod, what a stupid way to do the Agenda, the way I wrote it! You can't just tell people to pass, you have to give them a chance to talk about the business they've done with other people! It's absolutely critical!

That's when we started our first new BNI tradition — the testimonial. It was the first thing that we changed in the Agenda, and we did it almost immediately. From that point on, if you didn't have a referral to give, you didn't just pass. Instead, you gave a brief testimonial about the business you'd done with some other member of the group. That way, your experiences would become my experiences, and I could refer the member to somebody else. An instant referral multiplier! And we discovered it almost by accident. This was the first of many BFOs we've had in BNI. (That's "blinding flash of the obvious," in case you were wondering.)

You see, when I designed the original meeting Agenda, I had set up a process that was very efficient, but not as effective as it could be. The most efficient thing to do, if you didn't have a referral, was to pass — keep the meeting moving along, snap snap. But in terms of referrals, which is what I should have been thinking of, I learned that it was more important to be effective than to be efficient. Without testimonials, we had been missing a great opportunity to generate referrals.

I know from personal experience how effective a testimonial can be. Not long after we started this tradition, someone stood up at a meeting and said, "Dr. LaBriola gives the closest thing to a painless shot I've ever had." Someone else said, "Really? He really gives the closest thing to a painless shot?" "Yes, he really does." "Well, then, I'll go see him." And it sold me, too. I went to see Jim LaBriola, and he's been my dentist ever since. He's even become my children's dentist.

YEAR OF LESSONS

In sum, we learned two important principles in our first year of vigorous growth. One was that we had to focus on maintaining our traditions, our procedures, and our standards as we added new chapters and spread farther and farther from the main office, and that the way to do this was to train, train, retrain, and train some more. We would train new members so they would hit the ground running and become better marketers. We would train our Leadership Teams to conduct chapter meetings and operations in ways that we had found, through trial and error, worked best. We would retrain regularly to keep the organization working the same everywhere on the map.

The second principle was that we would consider every suggestion for change on its own merits. If an idea worked in one chapter, we would try it in other chapters, then in new regions. A good idea would then become a part of our standard operating procedure — a new tradition. This would keep us flexible, effective, and healthy. BNI might get very big, but it would not become a dinosaur.

STEADY GROWTH
1986–1989

TWENTY CHAPTERS IN ONE YEAR! I HAD NOT FORESEEN THIS, AND IN SOME ways our first year became one not of planning growth but of coping with it, trying to stay ahead of it. I was still a full-time consultant — at least that's what my business card said — but I was spending more and more time opening and visiting new chapters, hiring directors, staffing and running a small main office, fielding questions, and solving problems.

But my life was only beginning to get interesting. By the end of our second year, 1986, BNI was up to 40 chapters and into its second state, Arizona. A year later, we reached 60, and the word "national" was beginning to echo in my mind.

I was still staying personally involved in every BNI event I could manage to attend, but by this time I had hired Regional Directors to help form core groups and get new chapters organized and ready to kick off. In 1986 we had four Regional Directors in Southern California and one in Phoenix, Arizona. In 1987 we opened in Hawaii.

Three states in three years! I was surprised and amazed. Of course, now we open entire countries faster than that, but there's nothing like the joy of planting that first seed and having to jump back to watch it grow.

We kept adding chapters at this pace, about 20 per year, throughout 1988 and 1989. States were another story. We opened Montana in 1988. Then, in 1989, we suddenly expanded into four new states: Indiana, Nevada, Oregon, and Texas. After four states in four years, we opened four states in one year. It was like moving out of a small house, to which we had been adding rooms as the family grew, into a new, larger house with lots of big rooms for future growth.

IDEAS THAT WORK

Our first year showed us that a new idea could come out of nowhere, often as a BFO (blinding flash of the obvious), and become an essential part of what made BNI a success. Testimonials were the first example.

In 1986 we tried out other new ideas. Three of them worked well, quickly became standard practice, and led to unexpected heights of personal and organizational success.

A chiropractor in our Pasadena chapter was missing too many meetings and showing up late for others. We sent her our standard letter, telling her that if she continued to miss meetings, we would be forced to open her classification.

The chiropractor said, "I'm just horrible in the mornings, but please don't open my classification, because I get so much business from BNI. Can we work something out?"

The chapter leaders called me and said, "We have a problem with this chiropractor, but there's no written policy on tardiness. What can we do?"

"Is she a good member otherwise?" I asked. "A good doctor?"

"Yes, we like her a lot, but she can't be a good networker if she doesn't show up."

"Why don't you suggest to her that she have someone in her office represent her at each meeting? She can miss as many meetings as she wants, as long as someone's there to represent her business at 7 a.m. each week."

The chiropractor liked the idea. "I have this great chiropractic assistant, Elisabeth Prevo, who is really dynamic, and I think you guys would like her. Can she represent me at the meetings?"

Some people don't like meeting every week, so in our early days, as an experiment, we opened seven chapters that met every other week. Over time we found that these groups passed 52 percent *fewer* referrals than the groups that met weekly. We said to them, "If we can show you *one* thing that will double the number of referrals in your group, will you do it?" Six said yes. "Meet every week," we told them, and to their credit, they successfully made the change. The seventh was closed within six months.

The chapter leaders said they would give it a try.

So Elisabeth came to a meeting. When her turn came, she stood up and gave a terrific 60-second commercial for the chiropractor, and later she passed some referrals. Knocked 'em out of the ball park.

They said, "She'll do just fine." They liked her so much, in fact, that four weeks later they made her President of the chapter. She had graduated from being a fill-in to becoming a member in her own right, and a chapter officer.

I couldn't help noticing, when she came to a training session, that she was one of our more articulate and attractive chapter Presidents. But that's another story.

The second idea of 1986 was one that took a large weight off my shoulders. I had a difficult decision to make in the organization's second year that would have important consequences for BNI's future. Rather than tackle this issue unilaterally, I decided to call on the wisdom and insight of an advisory task force, later to become the Board of Advisors. This was a move I've never had cause to regret, for reasons I'll explain later.

Here's one more example of how great ideas can surprise you—and make you wonder, Why didn't I think of that? Sometime in our second year, a woman called the main office and asked about joining BNI. I named a nearby chapter and suggested she visit.

About three weeks later, I happened to bump into this woman at a

In the early years, I was probably one of the worst directors Ivan could have ever had, because I questioned everything. I am a right-brain person. I had a creative business. Structure didn't work for me. I said, "Ivan, you're in California — we do things differently in Connecticut."

I told Ivan I had a chapter that wanted to change its meeting time from 7:00 a.m. to 7:15 a.m. because everybody was coming in late. Ivan asked me, "What is the result you want to accomplish?" To get everybody there on time, I told him. "Okay, you can try it," he said, "but I want you to track the results so we can see how well it works."

The chapter agreed. They kept records of when members arrived. After three weeks they called me and said that they were going back to 7 a.m. Why? Because now everybody was coming in 15 minutes later than before.

I had learned two things from Ivan: the value of tracking and documenting the results of our actions, and the fact that when it comes to business, we're all the same.

—Alice Ostrower
Executive Director, BNI Connecticut

chamber of commerce mixer. I asked her if she had joined BNI. She said she had, but named a different chapter. I asked her why she had not joined the first, which not only was closer to where she lived and worked but was larger and passed more referrals every month.

"I visited that chapter," she said, "but I didn't feel I belonged there. I walked in, looked around, and wasn't quite sure what to do. They took my money for breakfast, of course, but after that, nobody spoke to me. They all seemed to like each other a lot, but nobody reached out to me. I felt as though I were interrupting other people's conversations. Finally, the President started the meeting, and I sat down and watched. When it was over, everybody got up and went back to their groups, and still nobody spoke to me. So I left.

"Somehow that didn't feel right to me, so I decided to try one other chapter. This time, when I walked through the door, there was a woman standing there who shook my hand and thanked me for coming to visit her chapter. She gave me a little paper badge with my name on it. She introduced me to several members, and they thanked me for coming and asked me about my business.

"When the meeting was over, the woman who had greeted me thanked me again for visiting and asked if I had any questions. I said I was interested. She sat down with me and explained how BNI works. Then she invited me to join.

"I joined them without even thinking twice. I felt like I was really welcome there.

"I know it's a smaller chapter than the one you steered me to, but I'd like to make a prediction. I predict that, within a year, the chapter I joined will be bigger and better than the first one I visited."

Not long after that, I paid a surprise visit to this woman's chapter, and sure enough, I was greeted at the door by a person wearing a badge that said Visitor Host. I learned that the idea had come from a member who had seen it used at another organization he was active in. It was

In 1986, I came up with this motto, which is now familiar to BNI members: "It's not 'net-sit' or 'net-eat,' it's 'net-work.'" I posted this saying on signs around the room for the mixer portion of BNI's first regional event in 1986. Having been to too many chamber and other business events where people forgot that these events were about networking, I thought this would help them remember.

such an obviously great idea that before long we were having every BNI chapter designate a Visitor Host and making it part of our training.

The woman's prediction? Yes, it came true. Within the year, her chapter had pulled ahead in membership and referrals.

A TALE OF TWO CITIES

We started 1987 with a two-state reach that was confined to Southern California and the Phoenix area. The next logical place to go, I figured, was Northern California. To drum up business, I flew to San Francisco and participated in a trade show. That's where I began to learn that it would take more than brochures to sell my idea.

BNI lacked concept recognition. I would show my literature to visitors and start to explain what BNI was about, and someone would say, "Is this like the Rotary Club?" or "This is just Amway with a new name, isn't it?" or "Oh, I get it, this is kind of like the chamber of commerce, but you're limiting the number of people." I found this very frustrating.

I talked and talked, and finally I talked someone into trying it. The light didn't go on, he didn't jump at it, but I got this guy to agree to sign on as my director for the San Francisco region. I trained him and sent him out to pioneer this vast new domain. He tried, and we talked, and he tried some more, and I flew up a few more times, and he tried again. But it was all for nothing. He failed to get even a single chapter off the ground.

This experience taught me a fundamental truth about building the kind of organization I wanted. I learned that you have to **look for people, not places or professions.** If you find the right people, the places and professions will come. However, I was soon to learn that they might not come in the order you might expect.

You can't just go into a new area and recruit people to implement your ideas for you. You have to find people who have the fire in their belly. They have to visit a chapter, at least once, and see it in action. They have to go, "Wow, this is great!" If you don't get that reaction, you won't get them to run with the program.

I went to Kalispell, Montana, in 1988 to kick off one of our first chapters in that state. It was a long flight to a small community, maybe eight or ten thousand people in the area then, and no guarantee that a chapter would take hold and grow. I went there because Bill Redmond had visited a BNI chapter with his daughter in Arizona, and he had liked it so much he had gone back home to Montana and put together a core group in Kalispell.

Now, if you had asked me early in 1987, "Ivan, where will BNI happen first, San Francisco or Montana?" I would have looked at you and wondered silently about your sanity. But by 1988 I had learned that planning and logic often take a back seat to commitment and passion. That's why I was flying to Montana instead of San Francisco.

In Kalispell, Bill had brought 25 or 30 interested people to a meeting room. He introduced me to the group, and I spent the next hour telling them how BNI worked. Now, by this time I had done about 50 Kickoffs in three states, and I had learned to read my audience and recognize when the light went on and they got the concept. Here in Kalispell, on this Kickoff night, I talked and I talked but the light did not go on. They just looked at me like, What is this?

So I finished my talk and asked if they had any questions. And this guy — I'll call him Frank — ignored me but looked over at Bill Redmond and drawled, "Bay-ull? What the hay-ull we gotta come here every week for these meetings? Look, man, we got a referral for each other, pick up the phone and call each other. We don't have to come to these damn meetings."

I tell visitors to look at membership as though they're being invited to apply for a position in a new company. We have business to give to a florist, chiropractor, dentist, whatever their profession is, and we need to make sure we invite the right people to give our referrals to.

—John Meyer
Executive Director
BNI Ohio

And I thought, Oh, man, I flew five hours to Kalispell, Montana, to explain how this works and this guy says why meet, let's just give each other referrals.

But Bill looked over at the guy and said, "Frank, how long have we known each other?"

Frank said, "Oh, about 15 years."

"In 15 years," said Bill, "how many referrals have you given me, Frank?"

"Uh . . . well, I don't think I've given you any."

"And in 15 years, how many referrals have I given you?"

"Well, shoot, you ain't given me any either, Bill."

And Bill said, "Frank, that's why we gotta get here every week and go through this, because otherwise, you know, we're all a bunch of friends but we're not helping each other in business."

And Boom! The light went on. The whole group — you could see the spark. And it happened because of Bill, not because of me. Bill was somebody they trusted. I'm just some city slicker from El Lay, trying to sell something they had never seen before. Bill had lived there all of his life, was well known in the community, had seen BNI in action, and when he stood up and said, "Look, this is the way we've got to do it," it became the thing to do.

In hindsight, it's obvious, isn't it? When I flew to San Francisco and tried to sell BNI to strangers, in essence I was cold-calling. But when Bill Redmond visited his daughter and saw her BNI chapter in operation, then called and asked me if he could open Montana for BNI, then closed the sale to his friends right there in front of me — that was networking, pure and simple.

BNI is a networking organization — and from its earliest days to right now, networking is how BNI lives, breathes, and grows.

NEW CHAPTERS

Twenty chapters a year for the first three years. That's still a record — mostly because BNI was small. I helped kick off every one of those chapters with a personal welcome to our new BNI members.

Of course, the Kickoff is only the final stage of forming a new BNI chapter. What usually happens first is that the director, having accumulated a number of membership requests from people unable to join because of conflicts with current members' professions, invites some or all of them to start a new chapter. They form a core group, which today is about 15 people but in the early days could be as few as three.

A core group member starts out with one distinct advantage. Remember, the rule is, only one member per profession — but a core group member is guaranteed a spot when the chapter opens. That's how we get people to sign up for the core group: we tell them, "Look, even if your competitor shows up, you're in." Usually, though, that's only one of the reasons a motivated networker decides to join a BNI core group.

Core group members also have special responsibilities that include making sure enough new members sign up to form a healthy, referral-generating chapter. We tell them that in order to hold their spot, they have to make a commitment to bring people to the group. The group's final task is to get at least 40 to 60 prospective members to attend the Kickoff meeting. This gives them a pretty good shot at signing up enough new members to form a group of *minimum* effective operating size, about 20 to 25. Getting 15 to 20 new people to sign up *in addition to* the core group means getting 30 or 40 visitors to show up. And to do that, they need to invite 80 or more.

Getting RSVPs from 3 or 4 interested prospects each doesn't sound like a difficult job for 15 or 20 motivated networkers, does it? If you want to know just how much work it really involves, you should try it. Out of 20 people who promise to attend on penalty of giving up their firstborn child, 10 will show up. You'll come away with a new respect for the special people who start a chapter from the ground up.

Once the core group is formed, you start their training. You do this by telephone at first; later, in the last few days before the Kickoff, you go there and train them in person.

The training manual lays out in detail how the Kickoff meeting is conducted. Though it may vary according to the personality of the director who's conducting it, the Kickoff generally covers several prescribed areas. You welcome visitors. You tell them what BNI is all about, how it works, what the benefits are. You talk about BNI's history and traditions, its core principles and procedures. You make it clear that they're expected to attend regularly

---

It usually takes six to eight weeks to get a chapter off the ground. However, one time when I was visiting in Hawaii, a person came to me and said she wanted to do a Kickoff. I said, "Great! Work with the director. It'll take about six to eight weeks."

She said, "No, no, I think I can do it faster."

"Okay, well, faster's fine."

"When are you leaving?" she asked.

"I'm leaving in two days."

"Well, I want to do it before you leave, because I want you to do the Kickoff."

"I don't think you can put together a group in a day."

She said, "I'll have 20 people or more here tomorrow."

And she did. And almost all of them signed up, which was a lot more than average.

She took it from query to Kickoff in one day — a record that's unlikely to be broken. And she was a core group of one.

and bring referrals. You tell stories and give examples of how and why these policies work. You answer questions.

One of the most effective things you can do at a Kickoff is to pass referrals. Core group members should come prepared to show visitors just how much business can be done in the group. It doesn't matter if the referral happened two weeks ago — the time to share it is at the Kickoff meeting: "I gave a referral to my colleague Joe a couple of weeks ago, and I just wanted to report it today," Only 15 core members, the chapter hasn't even kicked off yet, and they're passing 20 or 30 referrals! Showing is 10 times better than telling.

Often a new chapter is started by someone who has moved into the area after having been in another chapter. Having that person give a testimonial about BNI can be one of the most powerful recruiting tools you can deploy. You could stand and talk for an hour to visitors about why they should join BNI, but it can't match the power of a two-minute endorsement by someone they know — like Bill Redmond in Montana.

Not least, you talk about BNI's guiding philosophy.

THE PHILOSOPHY

When we started our first chapter in 1985, it was our mutual understanding that we existed primarily to generate more business through referrals. We also understood that a strong, productive referral network could survive and thrive only by rewarding all its members with referrals.

Therefore, we reasoned, the most effective way to show new and prospective members how powerful the groups could be was to give them as many good referrals as possible as quickly as possible. This meant that each member must go into the organization with one thing uppermost in his or her mind: What can I do to help other members?

The first thing new members were taught was this: "The way to build your business is by helping other people build their business."

BNI's philosophy of networking is simple: help others to succeed and you will be successful. Networking is not a method for only a select few, but rather a formula for success for anyone who is willing to help others succeed.

—Nancy Giacomuzzi
Executive Director
BNI Minnesota

We knew that instilling such a healthy, positive vision throughout our organization would have immeasurable benefits.

The logic was self-evident. And the philosophy was certainly not new to BNI. It was, after all, the basis of a universal ethic, common to all religions, a fairness imperative that underlies morality in all cultures — the Law of Reciprocity. This law has been expressed many ways:

- "As ye would that men should do to you, do ye also to them likewise."

- "No one of you is a believer until he desires for his brother that which he desires for himself."

- "Regard your neighbor's gain as your gain, and your neighbor's loss as your own loss."

- "Ask not what your country can do for you — ask what you can do for your country."

- "What goes around comes around."

When we first started BNI, we had a hokey phrase we used, kind of an unwritten loyalty oath: "I promise I'll refer you, you promise you'll refer me." Well, that was a little too complicated, and it certainly wasn't memorable prose. The concept was there, but it didn't work very well.

I kept looking for a vivid, succinct way to express the Law of Reciprocity. Finally, I found it. At a seminar that I attended in 1986, a key idea I heard was this: "Conduct your life and your business with the philosophy that givers gain."

Givers Gain. This simple, two-word condensation of the Golden Rule struck a chord, and from that day forward, Givers Gain has been our universally understood, easily remembered corporate philosophy.

BNI's two-word philosophy is so clear and memorable that it makes BNI almost unique among large organizations today. You can go to any BNI gathering and ask members, "What is the philosophy of BNI?" and they will shout in chorus: "Givers Gain!" How many worldwide franchises do you know of where not only the owners and managers but also the clients can tell you the company's philosophy?

THE RUSH

Now, the final part of a Kickoff meeting is a lot like the Great Oklahoma Land Rush. You impress upon the visitors that a BNI chapter can have only one representative of each business type or professional specialty. You remind them that it's first come, first served. And that's when you start to get interesting reactions. For a brief time, "Givers Gain" takes a back seat.

When your core group invites prospective members to a Kickoff, you want to have more people there than you expect to have in the chapter. Ideally, this means two from each profession, and in order to achieve that, you have to invite three or four. Of course, the people in your core group are guaranteed membership, so they don't generally invite people from their own professions. But the others? Here's where you separate the bold from the bashful.

I remember attending one Kickoff where two real estate agents showed up. I talked with them and learned that they knew each other pretty well — they were friendly competitors. I said, "Well, gentlemen, are you interested in signing up?"

One guy looked at the other and said, "I don't know, what are you going to do?"

The other guy said, "I don't know, what are you going to do?"

The first guy said, "Well, I need to think about it for a while."

And the second guy said, "Yeah, I need to think about it, too."

I was surprised. Usually, in a situation like this, both sign up, and the Membership Committee has to choose.

The first guy said, "Well, I'm running late for a meeting, I gotta take off," and left.

No sooner had he gone through the door than the second real estate agent turned to me and said, "You know, I've thought about it, and I'm going to sign up."

Now, here's where it gets funny. Two hours later, back in my hotel room, I got a call from the other guy. "Ivan," he said, "I've been thinking about it, and I want to sign up before What's-His-Name does."

I had to tell him, "Gosh, I'm sorry, but What's-His-Name signed up right after you left, and the Membership Committee accepted him right away."

"That dog! Man, you know, I wasn't even out of the room and he was signing up," he said. "You know, Ivan, I'm always telling myself, You can't blink. If you blink on important decisions like that, you're gonna lose."

Well, the upshot of it was, he ended up opening another chapter. So he got what he wanted, but it took a lot more work — all because he had blinked.

That's why we like to have plenty of overlaps at Kickoff meetings. As often as not, these conflicts lead to new chapters. That's also why Stack Days work, because when we deliberately invite people from the same profession, somebody almost always signs up.

WHAT'S MY LINE?

Many years ago, at a Visitors' Day, I met a person who was very interested in joining. His name was Norty. Norty sold commercial lightbulbs — not the fixtures, and not any kind of lightbulbs that you can get at the grocery store or hardware store, but commercial lightbulbs that can't be purchased in most places.

Norty said he wanted to join BNI. I told him we had over 100 chapters but not a single commercial lightbulb salesman. Norty looked at me. He said, "So, are you saying I can't join?"

"No, not at all," I told him. "You're welcome to join, but you need to know that with more than 100 chapters, I've never seen anyone in your profession in a BNI chapter anywhere, and, well, I just wanted to make sure that you knew that I haven't seen it work for anyone in your profession. I mean, since you sell only commercial lightbulbs, members can't even give you a 'mercy referral'!"

"So basically you're telling me not to join, right?"

"Norty, I'd love for you to join. I'm just giving you my 'buyer beware' disclaimer — I don't know if this will work for you."

Norty said he definitely thought it would work for him. Besides, he told me, even if he didn't get a lot of referrals, it would give him a chance to make great contacts that he could use to help his clients, and that would help him a great deal. He turned in an application.

Six months later I was back in town to visit that chapter, and there was Norty. He asked if he could introduce me, something the director usually did. He read my bio, and at the end, he said:

"On a personal note, I wanted to let everyone know that I've been with my company for several years. For the first time ever, I won the national sales contest for the most sales in a quarter. The company is sending my wife and me to the Caribbean for a week, all expenses paid. And I just wanted to say that when I met Ivan six months ago, he tried to talk me out of joining!"

Since then, I've never tried to talk anyone out of joining because of his profession. That and other lessons have taught me that success in BNI is more about finding the right people than finding the right profession.

chapter 5

THE WAY EAST
1988–1990

BNI TRULY SEEMED TO HAVE A LIFE AND A MIND OF ITS OWN. THE NUMBER of chapters and members was growing steadily; new regions and states were showing up on our map at an accelerating rate. BNI was positioning itself for a breakout.

I was pleased that BNI continued to surpass my highest expectations, but in many ways it was like an unruly adolescent in the house, monopolizing my attention and swallowing up all my free time. I found myself buried in work.

Drowning in work, even work that I enjoyed, was beginning to take its toll on me. In late 1988 or early 1989, I finally saw the handwriting on the wall. It said that I couldn't continue to run both my consulting business and BNI.

Big changes were coming.

NEW REGIONS

One of the most fascinating things to me, as I have watched BNI grow and spread on its own map and timetable, is the way new regions spring up far from the established regions. Our mighty 1990 leap across the country and back is a case in point — although it was not the first time this happened, and certainly not the last.

We live in a mobile society. It's not uncommon for people to visit a BNI chapter for the first time in a location quite far from their home town. They're impressed by what they see. Or perhaps they join BNI in one region, then move to another region or area a few months or years later. They go out and look for the nearest chapter to join and find there's nothing within a hundred miles. They think about it for a while, and they end up calling me and asking, "What's it take to get a chapter started here in my part of the country?"

I tell them, "Well, here's the situation. Since we don't have any chapters in your area, the first thing we'd need to do is get a director. You can't start up a chapter unless there's somebody there to help you through the startup process and conduct the training that's necessary to run a chapter successfully. Now, the job doesn't have to be full-time, but the responsibilities of a director are A, B, C, X, Y, and Z. Do you know somebody there who might be interested in being a director?"

As often as not, they say, "Yeah, me! I might be interested."

"Okay, then, let's talk." In most cases I'm satisfied that they're enthusiastic about the idea and committed to making it work, and before long, we kick off in their area.

> You'll notice that I use a soft-sell approach. The hard sell would be if my initial response had been "First, we need a Regional Director there. How about you? Are you interested? You know what, this is a great business opportunity for you." And the typical response to this would be "Uh, I don't think so."

This is the story of our 1990 whirlwind odyssey from west to east and back, in brief. Remember how we opened up in Arizona in 1986? Well, in 1990 one of our Phoenix members moved to Nevada, called us about forming a chapter, and ended up opening a new region in Las Vegas. Next, a member from one of our new Nevada chapters moved to Connecticut, the same thing happened, and soon we found ourselves kicking off our first chapter on the East Coast.

What do you suppose happened next? A few months later, a member from Connecticut moved all the way across the country to Lake Tahoe — right back to California, where it all started!

In 1990 we also opened BNI regions in Michigan, Virginia, and Washington, DC. In each case, the region was opened by someone who had seen BNI in action or had been a member elsewhere and decided to open BNI chapters in a new part of the country. It was not the result of anyone, including me, hatching a master plan and moving pieces around on a big table like a bunch of generals in a war room. We let BNI grow and spread naturally, through the magic of networking.

NEW PRIORITIES

In the early years of BNI, I trained and kicked off every new chapter myself, which involved hours of training by telephone, then two or three days of field training leading up to the Kickoff. This process was something I took great satisfaction in doing. But when we began opening new regions, I knew I wouldn't be able to do them all myself, so I began delegating many of these Kickoffs to my directors. For a while, I continued doing Kickoffs myself for about half the new Southern California chapters, and for the first two chapters of every new region.

By 1989, however, as we approached the 100-chapter mark, it was becoming obvious to me that I could not continue to do two jobs effectively. Even though I was getting by with a full-time staff of one and had hired some directors, BNI was no longer a small operation that I could operate in my spare time. I was making a good living through AIM Consulting (which was actually the owner of The Network at that point — it was "The Network, an AIM Consulting Affiliate"). I enjoyed that business, but I couldn't take on any more clients and still have time to devote to BNI. When people asked me, "What do you do for a living? Are you a consultant, or do you run this BNI thing?" I would say that consulting was my vocation, but BNI was my avocation. I liked consulting, but I loved the idea and the process of BNI, loved seeing it generate so many referrals for other business people and me, loved watching my efforts to expand it succeed.

There were a lot of business consultants out there, but hardly anybody was trying to do what BNI was doing. Yes, a good business consultant could make a great living, but BNI was fun and rewarding. I enjoyed it, and it was helping a lot of people.

So I bit the bullet. I sold off my consulting clients to some associates and turned all my energies into helping BNI reach its full potential — whatever that proved to be.

LICENSING

Selling my consulting business enabled me to devote all of my time to BNI, but even a 24-hour workday would not have been enough to handle everything that needed to be done in this fast-growing company. There was plenty of managerial and leadership talent out there already; that much was certain. I had to reshape the decision-making process to share more responsibility and accountability with others in the organization.

With regions dotted across the country from coast to coast, centralized management was bringing more problems than benefits. When a situation arose, I had to fly to Arizona or Montana or Hawaii to deal with it. Now, Hawaii is a nice place to be, but flying out every time there was trouble tended to eat up the operating capital.

I knew I was going to have to decentralize BNI's operations, and probably ownership. This meant I would eventually be forced to deal with a hodgepodge of state-by-state franchising laws. Before that happened, however, I wanted to test out the decentralized ownership concept by experimenting with a simpler approach to local ownership — a sort of "franchise lite." So in 1990 I licensed directors in a couple of regions that didn't require state registration — Arizona and Montana. A Regional Director would own the license but not the business. If this worked, I would go ahead with the franchise approach.

It made a difference, all right. Under central ownership, the director would call and say, "We've got a problem here. You need to come out and fix it." But when problems arose in a licensed area, trouble calls from our directors went more like this: "I've got a problem. Can you help me fix it?" This was a subtle but significant shift. It takes a lot less effort to teach people how to solve problems than to keep running around solving all the problems yourself. We decided that franchising would be worth navigating through the maze of state and, later, international laws.

In a very short time, local ownership proved to be an even better model than I had hoped. It attracted bold, high-achieving business people to the company, and it brought out the best traits and talents in everybody. We began to see more and more "star" directors, people who set high standards for others to follow.

Among our noteworthy entrepreneurs since we began decentralizing are such directors as Dawn Lyons of San Francisco, the only woman to have opened 20 chapters or more in a single year, as well as Art Radtke (Virginia), Dan Rawls (Tennessee), and Jim Roman (Virginia), the only men besides me to have achieved that same distinction. Dan Rawls raised the bar for the number of chapters that could be opened in a region; his success made us take another look at the kind of market penetration BNI might achieve as a mature organization. Hazel Walker, who opened BNI in Indiana, quickly demonstrated her skills at setting up trade shows and conferences; we use her models for putting on special events when we train directors. Paul Gray of Montana holds the record for BNI's longest continuously running franchise.

And which directors hold the record for opening the largest chapters in the history of BNI? In the US, Dan Georgevich and Kathryn Lodal share the honors; Fran Lawson takes the prize in Canada.

BOARD OF ADVISORS

In 1990, we achieved a major organizational milestone: we had in place a fully functioning Board of Advisors that had either reviewed or written every policy that affected BNI members. The Board of Advisors came into being to correct a huge mistake I had made in my efforts to decentralize our decision making.

BNI had started decentralizing as early as 1986, when our first directors took over the process of starting and training new chapters. This took a load off my shoulders and allowed me to concentrate on training the directors and putting together new training materials for chapters and members.

I had intended to let individual chapters do their own marketing, including printing up their own brochures, buying advertising spots, and so forth, so I arranged for the chapters to retain part of the membership dues for this purpose. Sure enough, within a year each chapter quickly accumulated a pretty good sum of money for marketing.

But events at two chapters quickly convinced me that things weren't going as I had expected. At one chapter, the leadership decided to hold a mixer and invite a lot of people. I attended, along with 16 of the chapter's 20 members. No visitors. The cost of the mixer was $17 a head for hors d'oeuvres, a lot of money at that time. It was an awesome party. They had a great time. I stood there and thought, This is all our marketing money, and they're throwing a cool party. The purpose of the money was to build the chapter, not have a party.

A couple of weeks later, I was talking with the President of another chapter. I asked him how he

> The members and chapters want directors to make decisions for them, but our job as directors is not to make decisions; it is to help chapters and members make decisions based on BNI policies and the BNI code of ethics that, oh, by the way, come from BNI members.
>
> **—Dan Georgevich**
> **Executive Director**
> **BNI Michigan**

planned to use his marketing money. I suggested printing some bro-
chures and other materials. He said, "You know, Ivan, I'm a lawyer.
I don't know beans about marketing, and I don't have time to learn.
Marketing is your job."

I thought, He's absolutely right. Marketing is not the chapters'
job. The money doesn't do them any good. Either they don't know
what to do with it or they blow it.

But how to fix it? I could go to the chapters and say, "You know
all that money you've been putting in the bank? Sorry, you can't have
it anymore." But nobody was going to be happy about that. The solution would be worse than the problem. You don't want to burn down
the barn to roast the pig.

I knew I had to find some way to get that money coming to the
main office so we could centralize our marketing efforts. After giving it
some thought, I decided that I had to take a big risk.

First, I took out a personal loan, using my house as collateral. I spent
several thousand dollars to get some marketing materials designed and
printed. I recorded an audiotape. I commissioned a logo. I printed some
brochures and other materials.

Next, I called about 12 members, Presidents and past Presidents
mostly, in my 20 chapters. I said, "I've got some tough decisions to
make and I need some key members to help guide the decision. I think
you'd be a good person to have on this advisory task force."

Ten of the people I called agreed to serve in the group, and nine
of them showed up for the first meeting. I had invited people who I knew
to be respected, people who were reasonably diplomatic, who were
leaders in their chapters. I told them my problem with the marketing
budgets, and I told them about the party and about the chapter that
simply didn't know how to spend the money. "I'm perplexed," I told
them. "There's so much we could be doing. We could have brochures.
We could have an audiotape. We could have a logo." I began laying in
front of them samples of all these items that I had had produced with
the money I had borrowed. Then I sat down and shut up.

They started talking about it. Within 10 minutes, one of them said,
"You know, it's kind of stupid that we have this money sitting out here
in these separate accounts. We really should centralize it."

Another said, "It doesn't make sense to have each chapter reinvent the wheel. There's economies of scale. You could get a lot more
for the money if you produced the materials here for all 20 of our chapters to use."

You know what a learning curve looks like, don't you? When you're learning something or being taught, it takes a while to get up to speed, and your level of knowledge and ability rises steeply at first, then flattens out:

Well, what does it look like when you've got nobody to teach you and no idea what you're doing? Instead of a learning curve, you get learning steps:

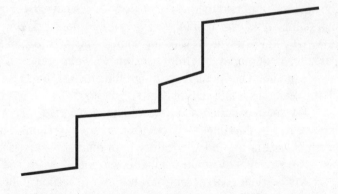

In this learning process, you go along, and Bang! You make a mistake. You bump into a wall. You learn a big lesson right away, and you climb up and start out again. You cruise along again for a while, then Bang! You're up against another big lesson.

Learning from mistakes is a fast way to learn, but it's kind of bumpy — and I've got the forehead to prove it. It has developed a flat spot from my decades of learning how to build an international referral networking organization. With thousands of chapters in hundreds of countries, I've made every mistake you can think of.

I told them I had considered that idea as well. I pulled out boxes of the items we had already produced. "Now, I went ahead and did all this material," I said, "hoping that we could come up with a solution, and I think that your suggestion might just be the answer. We'd get more bang for our buck, wouldn't we?"

This proved to be one of the most valuable exercises and leadership lessons I have ever been involved in. I didn't need to tell anybody what to do. All I had to do was lay out the problem, show them some possible answers, and let them come up with the most effective solution.

There was more to the problem than that, of course. I said, "Now the question is, how do we go back to the chapters and make this change in BNI without causing a full-scale rebellion?"

"You don't," they said. "We do."

We discussed the new policy some more. "Look," I said, "the last thing you want to do is go in there and say, 'You know that marketing money you've saved? You've got to turn it in.' That'll never fly. What we'll have to do is grandfather everybody. Let them keep the money they've already set aside."

So the advisors went to the chapters — not only their own, but all the others — and told them, "We've decided we have to centralize our marketing. Whatever money you've got in your marketing account, do what you want with it. Make up some T-shirts. Throw an awesome party. It's your money. But from here on out, we're going with the new system, and BNI has ponied up to start the process. Here, take a look at all the materials that BNI will begin providing."

It went over better than we could have expected. Of the 20 chapters we had at that time, only one put up any objections, and it, too, eventually came around. Centralizing our marketing efforts just made sense, and everybody could see that in the end.

My original goal, decentralization of our responsibility and accountability, had taken a big step forward. This was the birth of BNI's Board of Advisors. They worked hard, and they did a great job. They probably saved my company.

I saw immediately how a Board of Advisors could making running BNI vastly easier. I decided to consult them in all major decisions. I asked them to review all my current policies and make recommendations about which ones to keep and which ones to modify or drop.

This is what they started doing in 1986. It proved to be a daunting task, but by 1990, **every single policy in the organization had been either written or approved by the Board of Advisors.**

In its many incarnations since that time, the Board of Advisors has become one of the strongest leadership tools I could possibly have. The results have been much better than I ever could have expected.

Running a far-flung, loosely linked network of referral chapters, each made up of independent-minded, self-reliant business people accustomed to having their own way, is not a command-and-control hierarchy. It's more like herding cats.

But far more interesting.

A Life Partner

Remember the chiropractor's assistant I told you about, Elisabeth Prevo, the one who set the gold standard for fill-ins back in 1986? Well, as the man says on the radio, here's the rest of the story.

After a couple of years helping lead the Pasadena chapter, Elisabeth moved to Prescott, Arizona, and began working for a local chiropractor in 1988. She decided to try to form a networking group there to help the chiropractor's pub-lic relations efforts. She called me and asked if I would help her start a BNI chapter in Prescott.

I put her in touch with BNI's Arizona licensee in Phoenix. I also told her I would be happy to work with her personally as well.

The director helped Elisabeth start up her Prescott chapter but was not enthusiastic about having to visit a chapter so far from her home base in Phoenix. Elisabeth asked us both if we would let her run that part of the state. We agreed, and Elisabeth became a director. She did a great job of starting and growing BNI in Northern Arizona.

Not long after she rejoined BNI, Elisabeth asked me to come to Prescott and visit her chapter. It was a long drive from Phoenix, but I readily agreed. I was interested

It was a business din-ner, you know, and so every time he'd try to change the conversa-tion and talk about me, to get to know me, I'd turn it back to business. So finally he looked at his watch and he said, "I'll give you 15 more minutes to talk about The Network, and then I want to talk about you."

Six weeks after I moved back to California, we started dating, and six weeks later we were engaged.

— Elisabeth Misner

in learning more about this enthusiastic, energetic new leader — both as a BNI member and as a person.

Whenever I went to visit our Arizona chapters, I made sure to visit her. We began to see each other socially and went on a few dates. It wasn't long before I knew my interest in her was more than professional.

In 1989, Elisabeth decided a year in Prescott was enough. It was time to make a career move. She had job offers in Texas and in Southern California, and she asked me for professional advice on which would be the best place to move.

I told her, "I'm not the right person to ask."

"What do you mean?" she asked. "You're a business consultant. You give people advice all day long."

"My opinion is going to be biased."

"Biased? Why?"

"Because I'm interested in you," I said.

"I'll take that under advisement," she said.

She thought about it for a week or two. Then she moved back to California.

We began spending quality time together. After six weeks, I asked her to marry me.

Eight weeks after that, on May 26, 1989, we got married.

It was by far the best referral I ever got.

chapter 6

COAST TO COAST
1990–1994

THE EARLY '90S WERE A TIME OF GROWTH AND MATURATION FOR BNI.
We opened eight more states in 1991: Florida, Ohio, Washington State,
Missouri, Illinois, North Carolina, Alabama, and New York. In 1992,
we added Delaware and another part of Texas. Maine, Oregon, Iowa,
and Utah came aboard in 1993.

As our presence in the nation grew, so did our need for office space
and staff. Our first headquarters had been in my home in La Verne. I had
started overseeing the operation with a single full-time employee and
my sister, Lonie Misner-Feigerle, working part-time — the only person
besides me who has been at BNI headquarters all the way.

By the time I married Elisabeth in 1989, we were in dire need of
more people power. I thought of hiring new office staff, but Beth wanted
to work with me at BNI, so I gave her the first shot at the tasks that
needed doing. It turned out to be a great boost for our company. Her
skills, drive, and initiative kept our hiring needs to a minimum, and
her ideas later made a huge difference in our growth and vitality.

While Lonie kept up with the ever-growing task of assembling
and shipping new-member packets, Beth took on whatever other tasks
needed doing. And there were many: sending notices to Treasurers,
auditing and correcting reports, and a variety of member services and
development tasks, such as helping to develop our manuals. She took
over the editing and production of our newsletter, and she designed
and assembled an information packet for BNI. She began traveling to

other regions and states to open chapters and train directors. She ran the local company-owned region, which was BNI's largest at that time. We did have to hire new faces to answer the phone, which was ringing full-time, and to handle our growing shipping requirements.

We solved our space requirements in 1991, at least for a while, by moving our headquarters out of my La Verne home to a modest house on commercial land in Claremont. We also had to hire four new head-quarters employees to handle the growing work load and to take over the tasks that Elisabeth had been doing, because Elisabeth acquired a new job title: first-time mother. Our daughter Cassie was born, and our household became four: Cassie, my oldest daughter Ashley, Beth, and me. Two years later, our son Trey (Ivan III) came along to help level the playing field for the masculine branch of the clan.

A NEW NAME

The volume of business we were conducting, our geographic reach, the growing number of state and federal laws that we were subject to — all these factors were beginning to make the running of BNI more com-plicated and time-consuming. And as Founder and CEO, I knew that my personal assets were at greater and greater risk. To make BNI a true business, and to take my home and family out of the combat zone, I made the obvious decision. In 1990, we became a corporation.

This fundamental change in status had a ripple effect on our or-ganization. In 1991, we stopped calling ourselves The Network and became Business Network International, and not long afterward, for simplicity and for trademark purposes, just BNI. The "International" part was our vote of confidence in the future. Although we were still concentrating on opening new regions in our own country, we could foresee a day, still a few years away, when we would begin spilling across the borders.

As it turned out, we didn't exactly spill — we were pulled across.

THE CONFERENCES

Although BNI never stopped growing, we had a bit of a scare in 1989 when our rate of growth seemed ready to level out; that year, we added only 15 new chapters. I was concerned, because I knew the BNI model had great unrealized potential. The slowdown was also causing us budget headaches.

I asked Beth for suggestions on how we could cut expenses to make ends meet. She said, "Well, the thing to do is to fly out all the directors from the different states, put them up in a hotel, and train them on how to run this program more effectively."

I was stunned. "Uh, Elisabeth, were you and I at the same conversation? I asked how do we cut expenses, and you just laid out something that's going to cost us more money than we've ever spent!"

"Yes, I know," she said. "But the way to build a business is to do what it takes, and to do what it takes you've got to spend what it takes." She made a compelling argument that we had to make a major breakout. So we did, and that's how the conferences started.

In 1990, we flew the directors in — all 10 of them — and put them up in a hotel in San Dimas at our expense (this was before we had started franchising). We gave them several days of training in how to increase the size, number, and effectiveness of their chapters. The results were gratifying: our reach and membership started growing even faster than before. We followed up with another Directors' Conference in 1991, then in 1992 decided to begin holding them twice a year — May and November.

My first conference was Orlando in 1994. There were no registration forms. Meetings were not so much formal presentations as brainstorming sessions. Afterwards, we just hung out and talked for hours. It was like a small chapter of BNI, like a family.

—Shelli Howlett
Executive Director
BNI Dallas/Ft. Worth & Austin

The result was a major growth spurt. Over the next five years, we grew at twice the previous rate, hitting the 350-chapter mark early in 1995. Elisabeth's idea had helped get the company turned around and heading in the right direction.

FRANCHISING

To realize BNI's full potential, we would have to make our system one that could be replicated anywhere in the world, that would work the same no matter who was running it or where. This is the way a system is leveraged — by building replicable infrastructure.

The licensing we had experimented with in the late '80s had worked well. It had proved to us that decentralizing would make BNI a stronger and more flexible organization. But licensing would work for us in only a few areas; franchising was the only feasible way to go.

Franchising was about building replicable infrastructure. Each franchise would be a fully functional replica of the BNI system, on a smaller scale. Each franchise would have a full set of manuals on how to run the organization. Regional Directors would become Executive Directors when they bought their franchises. New Executive Directors would be brought to headquarters for extensive training in every aspect of the BNI system, based on our experience and the proven ideas of other directors.

We had learned a lot about training in our first few years. In the beginning, I had trained the chapter Leadership Teams, and each Leadership Team would train the next Leadership Team. But training can be like a leaky bucket; a little bit of water leaks out each time you pass it. With each leadership transition, we were losing a bit of our accumulated knowledge and understanding. When the original training program has entirely leaked away, your Leadership Teams have to make things up as they go.

I didn't want us to have to keep reinventing the wheel. This is why we had manuals. It's also why we needed to develop a system for training directors and Leadership Teams. We needed to focus more of BNI's resources and attention on training the trainers, who would then be able to train the growing number of Leadership Teams being created in new franchises across the country. It was the only way we could guarantee that our training would stay consistent and effective across the organization and through the years of growth that were ahead of us.

When I came on board, leadership training was an hour and 15 minutes, maybe an hour and a half. Ivan wanted us to build that up, and that's what we did. All of a sudden we had four to five hours of training for the Leadership Team. And then I had to overcome an obstacle. People are attracted to BNI because they can see how well it works, but when they're held accountable for their professionalism by going through the training, they resist.

— Margie Cowan
Co-Executive Director
BNI Colorado

We sold our first franchise in 1991, to Randy Borden in California. A year later, we had converted all our licensed regions to franchises.

In 1993, as BNI was becoming a decentralized, franchise-operated organization, we turned one of our twice-yearly conferences, the May gathering, into the Executive Directors' Conference, for franchise owners only. Our November meeting, the Directors' Conference, remained open to all directors, including the Regional, Area, and Assistant Directors. This allowed us to custom-tailor the training to specific groups of directors.

CONCEPT RECOGNITION REVISITED

As we opened region after region, we kept bumping up against a familiar obstacle: concept recognition. BNI was, and is, unique in its combination of operation, training, and philosophy. It was understandable that in each new region we opened, people sometimes had trouble understanding what we were about. They would try to relate us to something they knew: "Oh, you're like Kiwanis!" or "Isn't this pretty much the same as multilevel marketing?" No, we would patiently explain, we were not like any of those organizations.

By the early '90s, we had overcome most of this form of resistance because we had gained name recognition in the parts of the country where we had opened chapters. However, there were exceptions. New states often presented a problem, especially those with strong regional or cultural histories.

I'll never forget the time in 1991 when I kicked off a chapter in Montgomery, Alabama. Stacia Robinson was the director, and of course she knew the ropes well, but some of the visitors at that meeting were a little shaky on the concept.

I began, "It's a pleasure to be here in Montgomery — "

I was immediately interrupted by an older gent with a syrupy Southern drawl: "Son, you ain't in Montgomery. You're in Ma-a-awnt Gu-u-umry."

"Yes, sir. Mawnt Gumry," I said. "Thank you, sir."

I went on with my presentation, one I had given a gazillion times, a little shaken but none the worse for wear. As usual, I finished by asking if there were any questions. One lady raised her hand.

"It really ticks me off," she said, "when you-all come in here and tell us all about this networking thing and you don't just tell us it's Amway!"

"Ma'am, this isn't Amway!" I said. "And we're not a multilevel marketing company. Now, Amway's a perfectly good organization, but that's not us. We're a referral networking — "

"So you're not multilevel?"

"No, ma'am."

"Then I have another question," she said. "I'll bet next week you want us to go find a bunch of people and bring them to this meeting, don't you?"

I said, "Yes, ma'am, we do."

"See? Why don't you-all just tell us the truth, that this is a multi-level marketing group, but you gotta tell us it's a networking thing!"

At that point, I almost said, "You know what, ma'am? You're right. This is Amway. You don't want to be here." But I held my tongue.

I realize now that much of this particular kind of confusion came about because the multilevel marketing industry was beginning to adopt the term "network market-ing." There are many reputable multilevel marketing companies, but there are also others that are not so well thought of, and many people have been burned by fly-by-night pyramid schemers who take the money and disappear. This seems to be the case, even now, in every new country we open.

It quickly ceases to be the case, however, when people begin to see what BNI does and how well it works. As soon as they start feel-ing the satisfaction of helping their fellow business owners, as soon as they start getting referrals from their new network of contacts, as soon as the revenue from their new, high-quality customers starts pouring in — that's when they get it.

It's not unlike our experience with new technologies. Only a few years ago, such concepts as answer-ing machines, faxes, and e-mail

When we started BNI in my region, we just followed the book. Be-fore I signed the con-tract, I told Ivan, "If I'm correct in my under-standing of everything everybody's told me, you've got a system that works, and I don't have to reinvent it." And he said, "That's right, you just follow the system, and it works." I said, "Okay. I'm not interested in buying a franchise that I have to rein-vent." And I did exactly what they told me to do, and that's what happened.
— **Reed Morgan**
Co-Executive Director
BNI Central Tennessee, Central Kentucky, & Southern Indiana

were hard to comprehend. Now we use them every day without a second thought. And with concept recognition comes name recognition; not many years ago, Yahoo and Google were just noises you heard on a playground.

BNI is quickly building its own name recognition. It is also gaining a solid reputation worldwide, not as a get-rich-quick scheme but as a uniquely effective way of marketing a business.

COME TO THE DANCE

We like ideas to flow freely in BNI, from the field to headquarters, from headquarters to the chapters, from chapter to chapter and from region to region. Some ideas begin as experiments at the chapter level and end up being adopted across the organization. Others get started for use at the leadership level and end up in general use. A good example of the latter is an idea we call One-on-One Dance Cards.

The dance card idea sprang up around 1993 at one of our conferences. People came to Southern California from all over the country to attend Friday, Saturday, and Sunday conference sessions. Sunday was only a half day, but people who lived on the East Coast usually had to head to the airport before the conference was over. When the problem came up for discussion before one conference, we decided to hold the main meeting Saturday night so East Coasters could cut out early on Sunday without missing anything important. But what would the others do, the ones who stayed around on Sunday?

Beth and I brainstormed the problem. Beth suggested having directors pair up for interviews to share ideas or answer questions. Get a sheet of paper and schedule as many appointments as you could, she said. "Like filling up your dance card."

It was a terrific idea, so we called it Dance Cards. It worked great. It helped people make better use of their time at conferences. But at first people would say, "What the heck is a dance card?" so we changed the name to One-on-One Dance Cards to get the idea across faster. There's no idea so good that it can't be improved.

A couple of years later, someone asked, "Why aren't we doing this at the chapter level? Members ought to be using One-on-One Dance Cards before and after the meetings — during the week, and so forth." And this was obviously such a great idea — another BFO — that the chapters started using them right away. Now every chapter on the planet knows what a One-on-One Dance Card is.

We even designed a meeting stimulant around this feature. Half of the group are asked to put their business cards into a basket, and the other half draw out one card each. The two parties arrange a meeting during that week — a One-on-One Dance Card, in effect — and both have to tell everyone at the next meeting what they learned about each other. This often centers on their getting to know each other using a GAINS exchange, in which they tell each other about their goals, accomplishments, interests, networks, and skills.

The GAINS exchange is a terrific tool for finding common ground. Robert Davis and I wrote about it in *Business by Referral,* a book we published later on, in the 1990s. It's amazing how many things people have in common that they usually don't know about. At one meeting a number of years ago, I asked everyone to participate in a short exercise using the GAINS exchange. Several people grumbled about paperwork and wasting time and suggested finishing it at home and bringing it back at the next meeting. I said, "No, come on, it's only five minutes. Fill it out, then we'll go around the room and share it so we know a little more about each other."

They grumbled, but they filled out the forms, and we took turns telling our GAINS. Suddenly people were saying, "Omigod, you do that?" "You were there?" "I didn't know that about you!"

The clincher was these two guys who, I learned months later, hadn't said more than two sentences to each other in the three months they had been members together. They were in completely different fields, so far apart professionally that they were not likely to be giving each other referrals. Through the GAINS exchange, they discovered that were both soccer coaches at their kids' schools. They ended up becoming best buds, because at that meeting these two guys who had had nothing to talk about suddenly found they had a lot to talk about — and they started passing referrals to each other.

BNI is an immediate great fit for those who look at BNI with the right attitude. People who don't have this positive outlook generally either don't join or wash out quickly. The ones with the right attitude stay a long time.
— Kathy Morgan
Co-Executive Director
BNI Central Tennessee, Central Kentucky, & Southern Indiana

WORKING ON THE BUSINESS

One of the most amazing things about seeing your own organization grow from a small, local group of friends to a large company spanning the continent or the globe is watching it take on a life of its own. The systems you've designed are working as planned; you've got scores, hundreds of dedicated managers and leaders who keep their part of the system running smoothly; new ideas spring up almost spontaneously to be tested and adopted or discarded, making the whole organization stronger.

I enjoyed almost every aspect of my business, from running our headquarters, meeting and training new leaders, and designing new systems and resources to kicking off chapters and speaking to members at chapter meetings and Visitors' Days. But I was only one person; it was impossible for me to contribute much of value by concentrating on details that many others in BNI could handle just as well or better.

Sometime during the early '90s I began to realize that my efforts had to be redirected. I needed to turn from the familiar tasks of managing day-to-day BNI operations and assume more of a leadership role. I was already beginning this transition, of course, by decentralizing operations, delegating authority and responsibility, and turning regions into locally owned operations. In addition to farming out responsibilities and functions, however, I also needed to take a broader view of the organization from a higher perspective. Where was BNI headed? Which way should it go? How would we direct and manage its evolution?

Here's the thing about leadership. Think of your company as a large group of woodcutters whose job is to clear a road through a great forest. Like me, a lot of business owners enjoy the day-to-day routine of swinging the axe and moving timber. Their idea of leadership is often simply to get out in front and show everybody how to swing the axe. If it's a small organization, and if you know all your people, and if the road doesn't have to go very far, that's not a bad way to lead.

But if you're trying to build a large organization and the road is long and the territory ahead is unknown, things start to get complicated. You have to form teams to cut trees, other groups to move the logs off the road, still others to pile up the timber. You need engineers to measure the length and direction of the road you've built, supply personnel to replace tools that get worn out, accountants to handle payrolls and arrange vacation and sick leave time for your workers. All of this is important, but it's not leadership. It's just good management.

There you are out in front, several miles deep in an unexplored forest, chopping down trees and working up a good sweat and setting a good example for your cutting team. Meanwhile, somewhere to the rear, people are sitting on piles of logs talking about football and 401(k)s and how much better the company would be if they were in charge. Someone says, "You know, we should be doing something. I don't see much point in stacking more logs, so let's set up a lemonade stand and make some money." Someone else is wandering in the woods, looking for a shortcut through the trees, and the whole operation is slowly grinding to a halt. But you're unaware of this because you're way out front, whaling away with your axe.

To be a wise leader, here's what you need to do. You need to put down your axe, climb to the top of the tallest tree, and take a look around. You size up the situation, point in the direction you think best, and say to everybody, in a loud, clear voice, "That way!" You come back down and tell the cutting crew, "We're going to hit a ravine about a hundred yards ahead, and we need to bear right after we cross it." You tell the timber stackers, "There's a clearing not far off to our left where you can stack those logs and get them out of our way." And you draw up maps so everybody can see what's going on.

Yes, a leader needs to spend some time cutting and clearing and stacking trees and showing how it's done. That's called "working in the business." He also needs to spend time — the larger the business, the more time — climbing trees and drawing maps. That's called "working *on* the business."

I spent much of the early '90s working *in* the business, but by the mid-'90s, I was looking for new ways to work *on* the business. My search led me to some of the most interesting work I've ever taken on, and the results propelled BNI into a whole new world of growth.

chapter 7

GOING INTERNATIONAL
1995–2000

BY THE MIDDLE OF THE '90S, BNI FRANCHISES COVERED MOST OF THE
United States. There were around 350 chapters from coast to coast, and
new chapters were springing up at the rate of one or two per week.
The time had long since passed when I could help kick off every new
chapter, but now it was becoming almost a full-time job just to visit
each new region.

The expanding workload was making itself felt at BNI headquarters, too. New hires were needed to handle the administrative work.
We were outgrowing the little house that had served as our company's
headquarters office since 1991. It was time to move into a real office that
would give our growing staff room to work, to receive visitors, and to
stack and ship materials to our franchises, directors, and chapters. In
1996, we moved into new head-
quarters in San Dimas, a pleasant,
tree-shaded office villa that would
be our home for the next eight years.

NEW HORIZONS

BNI was a coast-to-coast operation
as early as 1990, but our sudden
leap from Southern California to
Connecticut left a lot of empty space
in between, space that we largely

filled up over the next five years. With our growth rate accelerating throughout the early '90s, we knew it was only a matter of time until we fulfilled the "I" in "BNI." Still, I wondered: Would BNI work as well in other countries as it did in the nation where it began?

The story of our international expansion mirrors the way we grew within the United States. It was rarely a matter of planning, of mapping out new territories to conquer; for the most part, BNI spread into new countries like dandelion seeds blowing in the wind and landing on fertile soil.

In 1994, Canada opened BNI's first new chapters outside the USA in Thunder Bay, Ontario. The transition was smooth; there was no bump in the road when we crossed the border. My anxieties were somewhat relieved. But would we find it as easy to open up in more distant lands? Canadian culture is not greatly different from what we in the United States refer to as "American" culture. As one Canadian member said to me: "Canadians are basically Americans with cheap health care and no guns." It was a good joke, but I still wondered if BNI would work in another country.

Our founding Co–National Directors in Canada were Don and Nancy Morgan. The Morgans were running a small business in St. Louis, Missouri, and were invited to attend a BNI meeting in 1995. They liked what they saw and immediately became members. They met the new Executive Directors, Mike Smith and Scott Simon, who told them I was looking for people to purchase a BNI franchise in Canada and rejuvenate the struggling Thunder Bay region. Nancy was from Canada, and she especially liked the idea. Don and Nancy came to California to talk with me and ended up purchasing the franchise.

What happened next was an amazing demonstration of the power of networking: Canada became our jumping-off point for crossing two oceans.

One of our early Canadian Executive Directors, Steve Lawson, had a brother, Martin, in London. Steve encouraged Martin and his wife Gillian to consider starting BNI in the United Kingdom. Martin and Gillian Lawson were at first skeptical ("Nobody in England even knows what the term 'networking' means!"), but they came to Toronto to meet the Morgans. They liked the meetings at the new Canadian chapters, which seemed energetic and well run, but still had their doubts whether members' enthusiasm could last.

They decided to come talk with me — and to observe some more chapter meetings. They fully expected to find our Southern California chapters populated with members who had been there only 12 to 18 months. Instead, they found chapters filled with people who had been there 10 years and were even more enthusiastic than their Canadian counterparts. The Lawsons kept hearing the same phrase they had heard in Canada: "BNI is the high point of our business week!"

They quickly became believers. Soon they were back in the United Kingdom to open the first BNI franchise across the Atlantic. Today Martin and Gillian Lawson operate one of BNI's fastest-growing regions.

Meanwhile, back in Canada, another of our directors, who loved traveling and was married to an airline pilot, flew to Australia and networked with local groups to open BNI down under. Coincidentally, a BNI member in England, Graham Southwell, moved to New Zealand and ended up buying that franchise. A visitor from Israel, Daniel Kutnick, attended a meeting in Toronto, returned home, and became BNI's National Director there.

From the United Kingdom, the Lawsons and their associates helped BNI open in Sweden, Germany, Switzerland, Austria, and the Netherlands. Spain, Italy, Malaysia, Singapore, and Barbados soon followed via increasingly interwoven contacts. One of our two yearly conferences, the November gathering, became our annual International Directors' Conference, and before long it began to look like the United Nations had relocated.

Flags of BNI's many host nations are on display at a BNI International Directors' Conference.

"WE'RE DIFFERENT"

Our experiences since Canada have taught us that there are two issues we are guaranteed to run into in every time BNI opens up in a new country. The first is the familiar obstacle of concept recognition; the second is a related mindset that we call the "We're Different" Syndrome. "We're not like the Americans," people say. "We have different customs, a different culture. We'll have to change things around to make BNI work here." This is often said with a dash of pride.

The Lawsons' experience is typical. "In the United Kingdom, we recognize the business achievements of Americans, but we're very suspicious of them. So it's not a good thing to tell a businessman this is an American idea."

It's understandable. Just like individuals, nations don't want to be told they're just like all the rest, but we tell them — and it's true — that referral networking, as practiced and promoted by BNI, is based on universal principles. People develop relationships with one another everywhere, not just in America. It doesn't matter if BNI got started in the United States, because **we all speak the language of referrals.**

In one of our early English-speaking countries, we ran into the "We're Different" Syndrome big time but learned how to make it right. Just as we had trained him to do, the National Director told his Leadership Teams that BNI transcended all cultural differences, that we all speak the language of referrals. They listened to him, looked at each other knowingly, and told him, "We're different from those Yanks. We don't do this, we don't do that," and so on.

The director called me and said, "I have an idea, and I need your permission. I want to change the manuals from American English to the Queen's English."

"Come again?"

"Well, we spell words differently here. Like 'organisation,' with an s instead of a z. We don't write 'checks,' we write 'cheques.' And our slang is different. If we modify the language a bit, people will accept it as a genuine national organization. Let me make some changes and show you."

I told him to give it a shot. At that time, our manuals totaled 200 pages (they're now around 500). He made 350 changes. I looked them over and okayed them. As he said, it was all word choice and spelling. Not a single procedure, Agenda item, or other material element was altered.

Then he went to kick off a brand-new chapter. He told them, "Some of you may know that this

The British hate to be sold to. If you're trying to sell BNI to a group of people at a meeting, Americans will listen, enjoy the experience, and say, "Okay, I'll do it," or they'll say, "No, thanks, it's not for me." Britons will say, "Oh no, you're trying to sell to me, stop that, I don't like it."

— **Martin & Gillian Lawson**
Co-National Directors
BNI United Kingdom

program started in the United States, but I want to tell you, this is not an American program. This is our own program. We have taken the basic American concept and put a spin on it that I believe, based on results, is working very well here. As a matter of fact, we made 350 changes to the American manuals. Here are our versions. Take a look."

They looked. They said, "Yes, yes, this is us!" That was the end of "We're Different" in that country.

We've used the same approach in every new country since that time. As soon as the members understand that BNI's approach transcends cultural differences and that the terms and concepts used are already familiar to them, they quickly buy in. The main prerequisite is that the country have a substantial middle class with a tradition of privately operated businesses.

I was first made aware of this fact while having lunch with Brian Tracy, the well-known business and personal development expert, public speaker, and bestselling author. "Business people are the same all over the world," he told me. "They're always looking for ways to do things faster, smarter, more efficiently, and if that's what you're teaching, they'll listen to you. It doesn't matter whether the ideas come from America or Germany or Japan, they're all going to follow the program."

It's not Americans doing business with South Africans; it's South Africans doing business with South Africans, Australians doing business with Australians, using ideas that came from America. The concepts transcend cultural differences and language differences, because the language of referrals is spoken worldwide. It's all about building relationships and system and trust.

The first time the UK National Directors came to a conference, it was totally a culture shock for them, especially during the awards banquet. It was our tradition that directors would line up and talk about what they liked best about BNI. It often got rather tearful and emotional. People cried because it changed their life. This was totally out of the comfort zone of the UK and Australian National Directors. Now they get as emotional as any of us, because they've seen the value, they've seen what it's done for their country and their lifestyle. It's an emotionally based business.

— Connie Hinton
Executive Director
BNI Seattle

The first countries BNI opened in outside the United States were other English-speaking countries, but other languages have since become commonplace in BNI operations. The first non-English-speaking chapter meeting I ever attended was in Sweden, where BNI is growing rapidly under the leadership of its National Director, Gunnar Selheden. Swedish is not like French or Spanish, from which English borrows a lot of its enormous vocabulary, so of course I didn't understand a word that was being said. About three-fourths of the way through the meeting, one member leaned toward me and said, in only slightly accented English, "Dr. Misner, you have no idea what he's talking about, do you?"

I said, "He's about to introduce the referral part of the meeting. Now he's explaining what a referral is and how to fill out a referral slip. In a minute he's going to go around the room and have everybody introduce himself or herself."

"Oh, you speak Swedish?"

"No," I said. "I wrote the Agenda."

Updating the Machinery

When I established the first Board of Advisors, I didn't foresee just what an important tool it would turn out to be in keeping BNI operating smoothly and responding to the needs of members and leaders. Once it had been formed, I not only referred all new member policy issues to it for guidance, I asked it to review all policies that were in place before it was formed. By 1990, it had completed that task.

In virtually all cases, I have been happy to abide by its recommendations. It solved a potentially serious leadership problem for me. Not only did it give me access to the judgment of savvy and experienced members, it spared me the necessity of defending BNI policies as whims of the Founder. When questions or objections arose, I could truthfully say that every BNI policy had been either written or approved by the Board of Advisors.

Changes at BNI during the 1990s brought two significant changes in my advisory structure. First, around 1990 the Board of Advisors became the National Board of Advisors, and later, about 1996, the International Board of Advisors, to reflect the scope of the membership now being affected by its decisions. The board provided advice and recommendations as needed to keep up with organizational issues and changes affecting members.

The other major development was the creation of the Franchise Advisory Board around 1995. This body would help resolve business issues and disputes among our franchises around the world. Not only did it relieve me of the burden of handling a river of contentious legal and administrative issues on my own, its decisions carried more weight — and were often much tougher and more hard-nosed — than any I would have been able to impose. Made up of directors nominated by Executive Directors and appointed by the Founder's Circle, the Franchise Advisory Board could say things to franchise owners that I could not diplomatically get away with. It also gave the franchisees an impartial body to which they could bring any perceived grievances.

New Tools

Our enormous reach put an end to one of the charms of the earlier, smaller BNI: the intimacy of knowing all the members and directors personally. When problems arose, they were relatively easy to talk out and solve in a small organization. Now that we had spread beyond the horizon, there was no way for this to happen. The International Board of Advisors and the Franchise Advisory Board are both vital to the smooth running of BNI but lack the caring, personal touch of those close early relationships.

To compensate for this loss of one-to-one contact, I asked BNI directors to help me appoint a smaller, more personally connected guidance council that I named the Founder's Circle. Three-fourths of this group would be elected by directors, the rest appointed by me. Members of the Founder's Circle would be my closest advisors, people I know personally or who, by popular agreement, had made significant contributions to the growth and operation of BNI. The Founder's Circle considers new ideas that might be tried out in small or large experiments. It helps the Founder formulate major decisions about the overall direction of the organization. The Founder's Circle is also charged with certain personnel decisions, such as appointing the Franchise Advisory Board.

There's more to staying in touch with members than simply getting advice, of course. I felt the need for hands-on help with my coaching duties. In a younger, smaller BNI, helping new directors get up to speed had not been a problem. After our new directors had been trained in the basics of operating their regions, I was usually available, either at headquarters or in the field, to address their concerns and help them get comfortable and familiar with BNI's way of operating. Our rapid growth, however, eventually made it impossible for me to cover all the bases, so I did something even better: I delegated.

I divided our US territory into five districts. In each district, I hired one of my most experienced Executive Directors to perform an additional function as the District Director. The main duty of District Directors would be to coach and mentor other directors in their districts. This move gave all directors ready access to the wisdom of our most experienced and capable people. There was a bonus in it for me as well: the five District Directors would help with business planning, member education, and marketing programs. They would save me hundreds of hours and thousands of miles of travel.

The District Director job was not a spur-of-the-moment invention. It was something I had been thinking about and planning toward for nearly 10 years. BNI's fast early growth had surprised me, but it had also made me think that perhaps I should be ready to hand over duties that grew too large for me to handle alone to people I trusted. District Director was just one of many new positions I foresaw; National Director was another.

BNI's worldwide growth in franchises, chapters, and memberships meant rapid growth in revenues as well. Our newfound affluence enabled me to fulfill a longtime dream. Beth and I believe each of us has an obligation to repay the community we live in, to share with it some of the prosperity it enables us to achieve. To that end, we established the BNI-Misner Foundation in 1998. Beth currently serves as the foundation's Administrator.

The BNI-Misner Foundation allows us to contribute to worthy causes every year, whether it is a lean year or a flush year. I asked the International Board of Advisors to poll our members and find our what causes they would most strongly support. We got back a huge list, but the top two categories by far were children and education. We therefore put our emphasis on mini-grants for schools in BNI countries throughout the world. We cover other bases as well — BNI chapters and the foundation donated $80,000 to the Red Cross for the victims of September 11, 2001 — but we always give at least $10,000 to $20,000 a year in education mini-grants to schools and individuals. The foundation also maintains an online presence at www.bni.org.

HIDDEN ELEMENTS

As an organization matures, its leaders must pay attention not only to the changes that need to be made, but also to preserving the structures and functions that keep it on track. Things that are being done right need to keep being done right if the organization is to remain successful.

There are actions you take as part of conducting good referral networking that at first glance don't necessarily seem that critical, but when you perform them effectively, they make a huge difference in the result. They take you to the next level of performance; they give you mastery. But the finer points of performing these actions well — including a deep understanding of why the actions are necessary — sometimes get lost in the rush to get things done. I call these the hidden elements.

There's a golf analogy I sometimes use to illustrate this point. The top 10 professional golfers in the world, on average, make about

$10 million a year in prize money and commercial endorsements. What do the top 10 amateur golfers make? Nothing. What's the difference in strokes, in an 18-hole game, between the top 10 pro golfers and the top 10 amateurs? Two.

That's $5 million per stroke.

Do you know how hard it is to consistently shave two strokes off your game? It's very, very tough, but that's what it takes to go from a no-money player to a big-money player. The only way to knock off those two strokes is to understand the hidden elements of golf — the grip, the stance, the swing, the all-but-invisible details that a professional golfer masters through unending practice, focus, and discipline. Only a very few reach the $10 million level.

I didn't understand the importance of the hidden elements until I was forcefully made aware of them one day in a karate class. My karate teacher — that is, my *sensei* — asked me to demonstrate my best *kata* — a series of moves that are like an imaginary fight against one or more opponents. What he said was, "Today I want you to *bunkai* a *kata*."

I said, "You want me to what?"

He said, "I want you to break your *kata* into its individual parts, and I want you to walk me through it. Show me each part and tell me what you are doing and why. I want you to do your best *kata*. One that you know forward and backward. One that if you did it at a tournament you'd win."

"Okay," I said. "I'll do Wansu. It's my best *kata*."

I started going through the moves, one by one. I performed a left forward stance with a down block. He stopped me and said, "What are you doing here? Explain it to me."

"It's a down block, Sensei," I said. "It's used to block an opponent's blow from this direction."

"Okay, take it to the next move."

I walked through the next several moves, explaining them as I went. "Good, good," he said.

"And then you come into a cat stance, like this, and then you do this thing" — slipping my arm upward through the air — "and then you go —"

"Whoa! Stop!" he said. "You do what?"

"Well, you know, you go into a cat stance and then you do this thing." I made an elaborate gesture with my outstretched arm.

He said, "Well, what is that thing?"

"Well, it's, you know, you're coming into the cat stance."

"Yes, but why do you do that?"

I was stumped. I had reached the limit of my understanding. There was nothing intelligent I could say — but I opened my mouth anyway, and said:

"Because it looks bitchin'."

My *sensei* — a sixth-degree black belt karate master, a tough, sturdy little man who could kick me up one wall and down the other — just stood there and looked at me.

Then he barked at me. He let loose a torrent of words, the gist of which was that he was less than happy with me. I thought he was going to pick up the phone and call my mother.

Finally he cooled off a little. He said, "Listen to me, Mister Misner. The martial arts have hidden elements, and if you don't understand the hidden elements, you'll never master the art! Every move in a *kata* means something. You have to fully understand each part of the move and why you're doing it."

Dr. Misner demonstrates a *kata* on UK Executive Director Robert French.

He showed me a move. "Now, what's the next thing you're doing after this?"

I said, "Well, you do this, Sensei." I demonstrated.

"And what is that?"

"It's a punch."

"Yes, it's a punch, but what are you doing with your right hand?"

"Sensei, nothing bitchin'," I said, "but I have no idea."

He said, "Look, when you throw the punch and you're in this position, you don't just throw the punch. You grab the guy, and *then* you throw the punch. It doubles the speed and power of the punch. That's what that 'thing' is. You don't do it because it looks 'bitchin'.' You do it because you're grabbing the guy. Now do you understand?"

He walked me through the rest of the *kata*, this *kata* that five minutes earlier I thought I knew cold. I learned it for the first time that day.

I learned what I was doing, how it was relevant, how it worked, why it worked. I took my first step on the road to mastery of that *kata*.

Later, reflecting on the life lesson my *sensei* had taught me, I began to realize how important the hidden elements are in everything we do. Over the years, I have tried to pass along this realization to the members and directors of BNI.

Mastering the hidden elements is vital in the art of networking. Every action that we train BNI networkers to perform has hidden elements that must be practiced and thoroughly understood in order to achieve mastery. It's also true in running an organization; the key to success is understanding everything you do — what, when, where, how, and why you're doing it.

chapter 8

A New Audience
1995–2000 (continued), 2001-2003

Between 1990 and 1995 I had thought a lot about how I might spend more time working *on* the business and less time working *in* the business. What were the most effective things I could do to help BNI reach its full potential? I could no longer visit every chapter. I could do a bunch of Visitors' Days and joint chapter meetings, but it seemed to me that was an awful lot of time and energy that could be used more effectively. I wanted to do something that would result in greater, more comprehensive, and longer-lasting benefits for BNI.

Over the years I had read a lot of books and journals on marketing, including most of the research that had been done on word-of-mouth marketing. I knew that this form of marketing, although one of the oldest and most effective, had been badly neglected both in published works and in business schools. In fact, I had already written one of the few books available on the subject, a 1989 in-house publication in a three-ring binder called *Networking for Success*, which had sold a few thousand copies. What I really needed to do was write a book that could be published and distributed by a publisher — a "real" book.

I found a publisher in Austin, Texas, who produced high-quality books — volumes that were carefully edited, well designed, and energetically promoted and distributed. In 1994, Bard Press founder Ray Bard, freelance editor Jeff Morris, and I began a long-lasting collaboration that would produce several more remarkable books and put us on the bestseller lists of both the *New York Times* and the *Wall Street Journal*.

It would also transform BNI from a nationwide network of hundreds of chapters into a worldwide web of thousands of groups passing referrals worth billions of dollars.

INTO PRINT

Our first effort was *The World's Best Known Marketing Secret*. This book was based on my research on the effectiveness of word of mouth as a marketing medium and on my experience with the many different kinds of networking associations. Although it wasn't a book about BNI per se, it was the first book in which I laid out the whole philosophy and rationale behind BNI. Among other goals, I hoped the book would both instruct and inspire BNI members to become better networkers.

The World's Best Known Marketing Secret was published in late 1994, but its effects, both large and small, began to be felt early in 1995. As I had hoped, one of the things that happened was that people began to see it on the bookstore shelves, buy it, take it home, read it — and then, perhaps, join BNI and make a difference.

This is what happened in the case of Art Radtke. Art scanned my book in a store in New England and thought, I should get this book, then changed his mind and left without buying it. It bugged him for a week. Finally, he returned to the store and bought it.

The book transformed his thinking. He thought, I need to join BNI. He found BNI's number in the back, called us, and asked to speak to me. He said, "I just read your book. I want to join a chapter in Cape Cod."

"We don't have any chapters in Cape Cod," I told him. "We'd have to start a new region. Do you know anybody there who might be interested in becoming a director?"

"Yes. Me."

So we talked about it, and Art decided to start opening chapters in Cape Cod, Massachusetts. Later he sold Cape Cod and opened another region in Washington, DC, and Virginia. Over the years he has been with us, he has become one of BNI's most successful and innovative directors — all because he saw my first book in a bookstore.

A Flash of Publicity

The other big difference the publication of *The World's Best Known Marketing Secret* made was that it opened a giant doorway for BNI to step into the public arena. This and our subsequent books gave us a way to go on the air and talk about our organization — for free.

If you've ever run a business, you know how hard it can be to get favorable publicity. The media don't want to interview you just to talk about your business. They will, however, interview any idiot with a book. If it's a good book, you'll get lots of interviews.

I've now done somewhere around 1,000 interviews for television, radio, newspapers, and magazines to discuss one or another of my books — and, almost always, BNI.

Of course, they still don't want to talk about your company. That would be giving you free advertising. But here's what usually happens: They invite you to talk about your book. At some point the interviewer says something like, "What led you to write this book?" and you answer, "Well, I run the world's largest referral networking organization. It's called BNI." The interviewer says, "Really? That's fascinating. Tell me more about BNI." I've had many, many interviews in which I spent the first 5 minutes talking about my book and the next 25 answering the interviewer's questions about BNI.

One broadcaster who has given BNI a lot of great publicity is Jim Blasingame, "The Small Business Advocate," whose radio show features interviews with entrepreneurs and owners of small businesses. Jim has interviewed me many times, usually after I've come out with a new book. You can listen to some great examples of these interviews by going online to smallbusinessadvocate.com. Click on "Listen Now," then look in the archives for "Networking."

The most memorable interview I ever did was my first live interview — which was very nearly my last live interview.

It was early 1995, *The World's Best Known Marketing Secret* was just hitting the shelves, and a cable station had invited me to talk about it at the County Exchange in Fairfield, Connecticut, right across the border from New York.

The interviewer called me before the show and said, "We'd like you to do something visual."

I thought, This is networking, not lion taming. What can I do that's visual? Run up and down the aisles handing out business cards?

So I put together a "tool box" with "networking tools" inside — badges, cardholders, and the like. Kind of goofy, but it was visual.

Somehow it didn't feel like enough. So as Lance Mead, the New York Executive Director, was driving me to the show, I came up with an idea. "Lance," I said, "what do you think about a magic trick?" I am an amateur magician, and I have a trick where I hide some flash cotton in my hand. I wave my hand, and a flame briefly flares up out of it. I happened to have my magician's kit with me.

"Here's what I'll do. We get to the end of the interview, the interviewer holds up my book, and I say to her, 'Careful! It's hot!' And I take it from her, and whoosh! Flames shoot out of it."

"Yeah, that's good!" said Lance.

A little while later, I was sitting in the green room at the studio. It was a large cable station, and the show was a big, 90-minute variety show with 10 guests or more. I was sitting there with Lance and a bunch of other people, watching the show on a monitor, waiting to be called, when this guy dressed like an Indian walked by. Then another guy walked by dressed like a cop. Then another guy, dressed like a cowboy.

Someone joked, "Gee, it looks like the Village People!"

Then I heard the on-air announcer say, "Next on the Fairfield County Exchange, the Village People! And Dr. Ivan Misner to talk about networking."

I panicked. "Lance," I said, "I'm gonna die here!"

I thought, Better spiff it up a notch. Make a bigger flame. I stuffed some more flash cotton into my palm.

The Village People went on. I watched them on the monitor. They were great! They were fun! They were hysterical! They did "Y-M-C-A," shaping the letters with their bodies, of course. The audience roared, screamed, jumped up and down.

I thought, If I'm going on after this, I'd better use a little more of the flash cotton.

The Village People kept the audience jumping and screaming for more. The show fell behind schedule. I knew my interview was going to be rushed. I was up next. I had the cold sweats.

The producer came over and said, "Get ready, we're going to have to rush you on and mike you up."

"Okay," I said. I took another pinch of flash cotton and followed him out of the room.

As the Village People came offstage to a rowdy standing ovation, I was seated in a chair in front of the cameras, half-facing the host and hostess. I was holding a copy of my book. I said to the hostess, seated immediately to my right, "Hey, listen, when we get to the end of the interview, would you hold this up? Then I'll say — "

At that moment, the director, who could hear us through her headset, walked over to us and said, "No, no, no, I don't want her holding the book up. We have a digital copy, and we'll show it in another shot."

As soon as the director walked away, the hostess turned to me and said, "You know, I'm the hostess, I'll decide. What do you want to do?" I started to explain the trick.

The director came back immediately. "I told you, I don't want her holding the book up! Okay, we're on in five seconds, four, three —"

The hostess whispered to me, "Just go ahead and do it. I'll follow along."

So we did the interview. I thought it was kind of a lame interview, especially following the Village People, but I knew we'd have a bang-up ending.

As we finished up, she said, right on cue, "I have here a copy of Dr. Misner's book." She held it up. The director scowled.

I said, "Careful! That's hot!" I reached over, took the book from her, and opened it up. And WHOOOOSH! a flame shot up. A big flame. A really big flame. A much bigger flame than I expected. The book caught on fire.

The hostess screamed, "EEEEEAAAAH!" and jumped into the lap of her co-host, waving her arms and hollering. The director was holding her head, yelling "Cut! Go to commercial!" The cameramen were coming out from behind their cameras. I whacked at the book, trying to put out the fire. The audience laughed hysterically.

Apparently I was a big hit.

The hostess, still sitting in her co-host's lap, said, "Oh, thank God I didn't swear on live television!"

Her co-host looked off-camera, snapped his fingers, and yelled, "Wardrobe! New pants for her, please!"

I looked over at Lance. Lance said, "We should go now."

Later, as we sped away in Lance's car, he turned to me and said, "Now, that was visual!"

I may be considered an expert on networking in most areas, but in Connecticut, I'm afraid they think I'm an arsonist.

Hitting the Bestseller Lists

With one book selling well and bringing us increased media attention, I decided to aim at publishing a new book every year or two. Next in line was another Bard Press collaboration, 1996's *Seven Second Marketing*, a smaller book focused on the art of creating a memory hook or catch-phrase to stick in the customer's (or contact's) memory. We published it because a lot of people who read *World's Best Known* liked the section on memory hooks and e-mailed me their own or handed me their card with it scribbled on the back. I collected hundreds of them, so many that it seemed logical to put them in a book.

Business by Referral, in 1998, happened because Robert Davis, a colleague of mine who is an expert in networking, brought me a lot of material on a highly systematic approach to generating and handling referrals. He had devised a number of innovative tools for enhancing networking skills, such as a variation of the GAINS exchange, in which networking partners swap information about their goals, accomplishments, interests, networks, and skills. Based on ideas he brought to the table, we worked out a three-step VCP system for building networking relationships through the stages of visibility, credibility, and profitability. If you think of *World's Best Known* as Networking 101, then *Business by Referral* would be Networking 301.

Next came *Masters of Networking*, published in 2000 as a leadoff for a possible Masters series, depending on how well it was received. I asked Don Morgan, our National Director in Canada, to help me compile and edit contributions from both BNI members and nationally known authors on the art and science of networking. *Masters of Networking* was designed to showcase the talent and experience of BNI's members and leaders, as well as authors whose names were already legend in the field of networking.

We had great expectations for this book. Having multiple authors gave us worldwide leverage; every contributor could promote the book and use local media to spread the word about BNI. On a single day, to be called "Masters Day," we would place our authors in bookstores nationwide and around the world. Our goal was to get *Masters of Networking* on the national bestseller lists. The publishing team behind this plan were once again Ray Bard and Jeff Morris, along with a new team member, publicist Michael Drew.

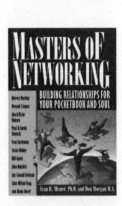

When I first heard this plan spelled out, I remember thinking: It's good to have goals. But it turned out to be a slam dunk. It was a promotional effort unlike anything the publishing community had seen, and it put us in the *Guinness Book of World Records*. Never before had a group of coauthors signed books in so many bookstores on the same day. It was a huge success, and it got *Masters* on the bestseller lists of both the *New York Times* and the *Wall Street Journal*.

We published *It's in the Cards* (2003) with Paradigm Publishing. My coauthors, Dan Georgevich and Candace Bailly, and I were intrigued by the creative business card designs we had seen among our members in this country and abroad. Starting with the idea that the business card is typically the smallest, most portable, most attention-getting, most collectible, and often most cost-effective of all a business person's promotional materials, we set out to make a colorful guide to designing, producing, and using this versatile networking tool.

Our next Masters series book came out in 2004: *Masters of Success,* from Entrepreneur Press. This was our first book not specifically about networking or word-of-mouth marketing — although the section on social capital certainly gave it a link. I had been concerned about losing the BNI focus, but our audience research had told us that a book on success, both in business and in life, would be of great interest not only to those who had bought our previous books but to a wider audience as well. *Masters of Success* would help make us visible to people who had never bought a

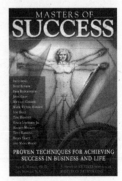

book on networking but who might be candidates for membership. BNI's imprint was apparent throughout; as with the first book in the series, most of the authors were BNI directors or members. We successfully promoted the book with another Masters Day and made the *Wall Street Journal* bestseller list.

Our books have become a vital part of BNI's culture. They have introduced the techniques, principles, and philosophy of referral networking to thousands of current and potential BNI members, and they have brought us the attention of a worldwide audience as well. The book you're reading now represents the first time the whole BNI story has been put down on paper.

All the same, I sometimes feel we rely too much on collateral marketing material. For our first 12 months, we marketed BNI with just one sheet of paper — the BNI Meeting Agenda, which I had typed up in a hurry on an old IBM Selectric (using the Columbus style of typing — "seek out and discover") and photocopied a gazillion times. Revisions were made using white-out and ball-point.

When people asked for a brochure, I told them to come to a meeting, because that was the only way for them to see what it was really all about. If they pressed for information, I handed them the Agenda (white-out, ink, and all) and told them, "This is what happens at a meeting, but you really need to see it for yourself."

It is critically important for visitors to attend a well-run meeting and to see the program working the way it was meant to. No one comes to a meeting because of a brochure or a video; he comes because you look him in the eye and say, "Hey, this is the way I get a lot of business, and I think you can get a lot of business out of this, too. How about coming to a meeting

Ivan and I were walking down the main street in downtown Toronto, and Ivan said to me, "I've been thinking about writing a book called *Masters of Networking.* What do you think?" I said, "I think it sounds like a really good idea." And we discussed it a little bit further and he said, "I've been thinking about asking you to be my coauthor. What do you think?" I said, "Well, yeah!" Then I calmed down said, "Thank you very much, I'm honored." That little event sticks out clearly in my mind, because writing a book was always in my plan.

— Don Morgan
Co–National Director
BNI Canada

with me?" No one joins because you give her stuff to read; she joins when she sees the Agenda in action. No brochure can show her that. I opened the first 20 chapters almost by accident, with nothing more than personal invitations and a typed, one-page Agenda.

Today, BNI has thousands of pages of support material — Directors' Manuals, Leadership Team Manuals, Visitor Host and Membership Committee Manuals, Chapter Toolkits, audio CDs, the books that I've written, and a myriad of collateral marketing materials. We've been highlighted in dozens of books by marketing experts and featured in hundreds of newspapers and magazines worldwide. We are, without question, the largest and most successful business networking organization in the world. But even today, the most important aspect of our success comes down to running a great meeting. That's where we shine, and that's what sells.

A FAST FIVE YEARS

What was behind BNI's phenomenal growth from 1995 to 2000? I think there were four main factors.

First, we had given BNI a solid foundation. We had a good organizational structure, capable leaders, and well-designed manuals to train and guide new generations of members and leaders. Our philosophy, Givers Gain, was intimately woven throughout the very fabric of the organization. Members were inspired to recruit more and more new members because the philosophy worked: the more you give to others, the more others give to you.

Second, we had started franchising, and franchising meant local ownership. Decentralizing our operation enhanced local focus and support, which are very important in networking. People are more likely to sign on as partners in an enterprise when they can own and operate their own part of it locally. And local responsibility took a lot of the work out of our hands. It freed up our time at the head office — time that we could use to look ahead, develop BNI's vision, and make strategic decisions that would stimulate more growth.

Third, we jumped our borders and began spreading from new centers. These new countries reaped the benefits of our years of domestic growth, development, and learning. Their rate of growth, in many cases, easily topped BNI's previous records in the United States.

Fourth, we made ourselves better known by publishing books, which opened the door to the world of media interviews. The public attention they generated gave our growth rate a real shot in the arm. From 1995 through 1999 we added more than four times as many chapters as we had from 1990 through 1994. We even added a new country as a direct result of one of our books: Singapore opened in 1998 because two businessmen, Sim Chow Boon and Mervin Yeo, read *The World's Best Known Marketing Secret* and applied to become National Directors.

By 2000, only 15 years after we formed the first chapter in Arcadia, BNI was catching on around the world and rapidly closing in on the 2,000-chapter mark.

A New Millennium
2001–2004

THE OPENING YEARS OF THE 21ST CENTURY HAVE BEEN A TIME OF GROWTH and transition at BNI. We've improved and fine-tuned our most successful programs. We've created new systems to support our growth. Having gone to a locally owned structure run by our 600 Executive Directors and their Area and Assistant Directors, we've almost completely phased out the position of Regional Director, which is now used only in our few company-owned regions. We've opened chapters in new countries and on five of the seven continents (South America may come aboard in the next few years, but I wouldn't count on Antarctica).

A worldwide business needs more space than we had in our pleasant but compact offices in San Dimas, so a move was inevitable. In 2004 we opened new headquarters in a beautiful, modern, two-story complex in Upland, not far from the tiny Claremont house that was our home 10 years before. Finally we have enough room for all our departments to spread out, especially our much-imposed-on warehouse and shipping staff.

Most of all, a growing business needs people who are smart, personable, and motivated. BNI has a built-in advantage in finding and hiring great people, because we do networking better than almost anybody — and we hire by referral. Somebody we know recommends someone we don't know for a position, and we are not surprised to find that those we hire are excellent employees who stay with us for many years. We've never had to advertise to fill an open position, and with such low turnover, we don't often have any to fill.

PEOPLE POWER

The folks who run the day-to-day operations at BNI are mostly people who have been with us for a long time and have grown with the organization. I am surrounded by able and dedicated people who keep me on a precise and efficient schedule and the whole organization working like a fine Swiss watch. They're all great employees, but I'd like to name those who have been at BNI more than five years.

Amy Turley-Brown, who is our Operations Director, was a chapter member representing a hair salon before she came to work at BNI headquarters in 1991. She soon began to prove her obvious potential. Amy is a classic example of a worker who is most concerned with doing a good job. We like to reward people with that attitude.

In the thick of one excruciatingly frustrating conference setup fiasco, Amy, who was then our Receptionist, asked me if I would like to never have to deal with these problems again. When I said yes, she took charge and put together, with no further cost to my sanity, the best conference we had ever held. After she did it again the following year, I gave her a well-earned promotion, the first of many. She has arranged every US National and International Directors' Conference since that time.

Our Support Services Supervisor, Leroy Gaines, organizes and operates many of our training, mentoring, and other programs. Under Leroy's supervision, headquarters operates in two principal modes. In our proactive mode, we work to fulfill our plans by updating our training manuals, producing collateral materials, and so forth. In our reactive or "fire department" mode, we rally to solve problems and head off crises as soon as they arrive on our doorstep.

Trish Holland came to work for us as a Receptionist and has since been promoted to Shipping Supervisor. Jamie Ball works as a Shipping Assistant.

Lonie Misner Feigerle, BNI's first employee, has been an essential part of our organization from the very beginning. She is now our Auditor and Technical Support Specialist, as well as the Senior Regional Director in Southern California, the company-owned area where it all began.

Elisabeth Misner, my wife, has been involved with BNI since 1986, now as the Administrator of the BNI-Misner Foundation. I find it hard to imagine what BNI would look like today without the balance, intelligence, and creative energy she brought to the organization at critical moments.

In addition to running seven franchises from his home base in Phoenix and serving four days a week in our Upland headquarters office as BNI's US National Director, Norm Dominguez is the Chief Operating Officer for our headquarters operations. Norm has been with BNI since 1987. He started off as a BNI member in Phoenix and became a Regional Director, then an Executive Director. Later, as District Director, he coached Executive Directors in the nine-state Rocky Mountain Southwest District of BNI and helped monitor and administer their operations. I honestly don't see how anyone else could have stepped up to the plate and knocked the ball over the fence the way Norm has done. His superb management savvy, people skills, and raw energy are enough for several ordinary executives. He is ably helped by his Administrative Assistant, Sue Thompson, who keeps him from running into himself coming around the corner.

THE COMMUNICATION REVOLUTION

The larger an organization grows, the more crucial it is to keep the rising river of information flowing smoothly. This includes keeping track of membership, revenues, expenses, and other data. BNI made a major step forward in 2002 with the inauguration of BNINET, our universal worldwide online database system. Rather than accumulating written reports as they dribble in, week by week and month by month, from around the globe, BNI now has a real-time readout of each chapter's and each franchise's statistics. This vastly simplifies our accounting, facilitates our operations, and helps us stay ahead of developing problems.

BNINET was conceived and developed in Great Britain by UK National Directors Martin and Gillian Lawson. When we saw how well it worked, we selected BNINET to be BNI's official database system and gave Connie Hinton, our Executive Director in Seattle and Chair of the BNI Technology Committee, the task of developing it for worldwide use.

Among other conveniences, BNINET enables us to distribute our online newsletter, *SuccessNet™*, to all members almost instantaneously. No longer do membership rolls and members' addresses have to be entered laboriously by hand at headquarters. This upgrade in two-way communication ability between headquarters and the field makes our network a fully functioning global system.

EXPERIMENTAL PROGRAMS

In an organization that's made up largely of entrepreneurs and independent business people, good ideas come from everywhere. This is a good thing to remember in any setting, but it's especially true in a company like BNI. You never know where the next brilliant idea is going to spring up.

When you run a franchise, you perform a balancing act between the stability of following a proven system and the importance of trying out new ideas. We know from experience what works for us, and we train intensively to keep the whole system working in harmony. But the day you say, "Look, this is the system, and you can't change a single thing under any circumstances" — that's the day you become number two.

I felt that the way to nurture both stability and innovation was to officially sanction experimental programs. Want to try something new in your chapter? Okay. Write me a proposal, and I'll sign off on it. Try it for a while. If we don't think it's working by the end of a certain time, you'll discontinue it. If it works, we may use it worldwide.

We have many examples of experiments that were successful. Educational Coordinator is one. This experiment was suggested by several people, but it was Norm Dominguez who made it happen.

Education and training have always been important in BNI, but until we acquired a substantial library of content, there wasn't a

As a new National Director in 2001, it occurred to me that a regular weekly workshop would be a way of adding value for both BNI membership and the Executive Directors in Australia — a proper workshop with instructions as to what to say and do, as well as what support materials you would need. After all, many of our Educational Coordinators did not have my 20 years experience in speaking and training. And the idea just grew.

— Geoffrey Kirkwood
National Director
BNI Australia

whole lot of networking-specific material to train on. Our first resources were my books, and over several years we put together a pretty good collection of other materials, including my articles on Entrepreneur.com, books from our franchises, books by people like Bob Burg and Susan RoAne. We recommended that everybody read these materials, but we didn't have any reliable way of making sure that this information was getting to the chapters.

Norm's idea was to assign an Educational Coordinator in each chapter to talk briefly at each meeting about networking and suggest books and articles for further reading. A few chapters around the country were already trying this, so I told Norm to go ahead and do it in Phoenix as an experimental program.

Norm soon began recommending that we make it part of the Agenda. I resisted. I didn't want to change the Agenda. "You add a couple of minutes here and a couple of minutes there," I told him, "and pretty soon the meeting goes on all day."

"You really should try it out in other areas," he said. "This is powerful."

Finally I relented. "Okay, if you like it that much, let's give it a test run." We brought it up at a Founder's Circle meeting; a few other directors agreed to try it. Everybody who tried it liked it. "We need to be doing this everywhere," they said.

That's how the Educational Coordinator was born. We tried it out in a controlled experiment, and it worked so well that we made it standard practice throughout BNI.

The Member Success Program is another example. In the mid- to late '90s, while we were implementing the Educational Coordinator program, we were telling each other that we needed to do more training for new members outside the regular meetings. John Meyer, Executive Director in Ohio, started holding a one-hour orientation program that he called New Member Mondays. Other directors started similar programs: Steve Lawson and Don Morgan in Canada, Martin and Gillian Lawson in the United Kingdom. It was such a success that word got around and the program spread like wildfire. The result was more effective members — people who were better at marketing their businesses and bringing in referrals from the very first meeting. Chapters that held New Member Mondays had higher membership and retention than others.

This successful experiment led to the Member Success Program, a 2- to 3-hour training session that is now required of every BNI member within a few weeks of joining. We decided not to call it New Member

Orientation, because it is designed to serve as a refresher course as well. We now encourage all members to take MSP every couple of years.

MSP provides the individual a foundation for being successful in the chapter. How do you put together and present a good 60-second commercial? How do you prepare for your 10-minute presentation? Why are One-on-One Dance Cards so important, and how do you use them? What are Meeting Stimulants, and how do they work? What is the BNI-Misner Foundation? The content varies from region to region, and we can't cover it all in a single 2- or 3-hour class, so we tell directors to cover what's most important in their regions.

This program is another example of what sets us apart from our competition. No other referral networking organization requires its members to undergo this kind of orientation to the methods, goals, and philosophy of the organization, and those that offer training charge members for it. We not only require it, we do it for free — it's covered by the dues — because we know it benefits every member and makes BNI stronger.

Some experiments work out a lot better than I expect them to. One good example is our Directors' Mentoring Program. When Elisabeth suggested it to me in 1996, I was skeptical. I've seen too many mentoring programs start with glowing expectations, only to fizzle out within a year or two. I didn't think even Elisabeth's resolve and organizing skills could overcome the odds against it. But I'm happy to say I was wrong. From five mentoring pairs in its first year, this well-designed, well-run program has grown so much that about 90 percent of new directors now get some form of mentoring from more experienced directors. Much of this occurs at the spring and fall conferences and is facilitated by use of One-on-One Dance Cards — as I now recall, another of Elisabeth's brainstorms.

CNP AND THE REFERRAL INSTITUTE

Because education is such an important factor in BNI's success, we constantly look for ways to innovate and improve our structured training. In the late 1990s, I realized that we needed a package of materials that BNI members could use to learn the principles and skills of professional-quality referral networking and word-of-mouth marketing. I had already created and accumulated an assortment of materials over several years, including *The World's Best Known Marketing Secret* and other books I had written. From these, Steve Lawson, an Executive Director in Canada, and I put together the first version of a training curriculum I called the Certified Networker Program.

I had been thinking that this kind of training would help our BNI members as well as be a good way to expose nonmembers to the BNI program. One day Art Radtke, a BNI Executive Director in Virginia, happened to tell me an idea he had about creating a comprehensive training program on networking and word-of-mouth marketing for corporations and for people everywhere in the world. I liked the idea, so Art and I became partners in a new company, which we named the Referral Institute. In 2002 we added Mike Garrison, Executive Director of BNI Southwestern Virginia, to our team. When Art left the program a year later, we asked Mike Macedonio, BNI Executive Director in Massachusetts and Rhode Island, to become a partner. These two gentlemen — we call them Mike Squared in honor of their exponential effectiveness together — are now the active partners in operating the Referral Institute.

The Certified Networker Program is a customized curriculum with tips, tools, and techniques to help BNI members — and anyone else, for that matter — become more effective and productive networkers. Refined and expanded, it is now administered by the Referral Institute as a series of interactive workshops, 12 in all, covering every aspect of a well-rounded referral-based marketing system (certifiednetworker.com).

Why didn't we make RI a part of BNI? We spun it off to avoid confusion about what business BNI is in. Although training is an important part of BNI's operation, BNI is not a training company — it is a referral networking organization, and it must stay focused on that purpose. The Referral Institute is a company that trains people how to network; BNI is the place where this training can be put to work. It is important to note, however, that RI has a strong strategic alliance with BNI and we know that it will always refer people to BNI.

MEMBERSHIP DRIVES

When a new chapter is formed, it usually grows quickly as the core group recruits friends and acquaintances. Once this pool of contacts is used up, however, growth often tends to slow. It's a common phenomenon with organizations. With BNI, it's important for chapters to keep growing, filling as many professional and business categories as possible, because the number of referrals generated increases much faster than the number of new members.

Early in BNI's history, several chapter Leadership Team members came to me and said they needed some help. "What's headquarters doing to help us build our membership? We need to have some kind of membership drive, something special that would motivate members to bring in new members."

I agreed. We tried an experiment. We asked members what they thought would motivate them to go out and round up new members. Free dues, they said. Bring in five people, you get six months' free dues, or something along those lines.

It was a miserable failure. We gained a few new members, but we learned that money was not the motivator we had expected, especially negative money — money that they didn't have to spend but would never see. Somehow that just didn't register as an incentive.

We tried a few other things, but the idea that hit the bullseye was travel. If you and your chapter brought in an impressive number of new members, your reward could be a trip to Las Vegas or Mexico or some other exotic destination. It was like a big lottery contest. Not everybody got a prize, but the top recruiters got a chance at winning a trip. The potential payoff was so exciting that people eagerly recruited new members by the dozens and hundreds.

Today, leveraged by the prospect of travel and adventure, our membership drives have achieved legendary status. Our champion recruiter, Executive Director Dan Georgevich, has turned the membership drive into a science. He gets members excited about bringing visitors and lavishes recognition on the winners. His chapters in Michigan once added more than 750 new members in a single Membership Extravaganza. We have entire BNI regions that don't even have 750 members.

There's an expression I use to explain the advantages of size: "The Power of 20." I once heard another director say that size didn't matter, so I did a study of the chapters in my region. I found that chapters having more than 20 members generated three times as many referrals, on average, as chapters with less than 20. So size does matter — the bigger, the better. My chapters in West Virginia now average 28 members, and they're some of the best referral generators in the country.

— Mike Garrison
Executive Director
BNI SW Virginia

chapter 10

BNI TRADITIONS
THINGS EVERY MEMBER SHOULD KNOW

WE KEEP THE CULTURE OF BNI STRONG BY CONSTANTLY TRAINING AND retraining members and leaders. In these training sessions, we emphasize BNI's traditions, because traditions help make a company what it is. **Traditions tell us who we are as an organization.**

It is also important for every organization to state its purpose clearly and succinctly, to communicate to its members and to the world what the organization is about. Here is BNI's mission statement:

> **The mission of BNI is to help members increase their business through a structured, positive, and professional "word-of-mouth" program that enables them to develop long-term, meaningful relationships with quality business professionals.**

All of BNI's traditions are tailored to support this mission. They are the expression and implementation of our basic principles.

I've always believed that any goal worth pursuing must be achieved through a principled effort — that an enterprise devoid of moral, ethical, and practical standards is doomed to eventual failure. I have been proven right over and over again by the actions and attitudes of BNI members and chapter leaders. It would be hard to find a more giving, more helpful, more positive group of people than can be seen at any gathering of BNI members, whether a weekly chapter meeting, a Visitors' Day, a Leadership Team training session, or an International Directors' Conference.

GIVERS GAIN

The central, guiding philosophy of BNI has always been the concept of giving benefit to others. It's an ethical theme that is common to all religions, all cultures: treat others the way you want to be treated. If you want to get referrals, do the best job you can of giving referrals to others. In 1986, we condensed this philosophy into two words: Givers Gain.

Here's what I say to every chapter that I kick off: "BNI is all about Givers Gain. This is the philosophy of BNI. If you want to get business, you have to be willing to give business to other business people."

Then I tell them a story that I originally heard from one of our top trainers, Art Radtke, who is also an Executive Director in Virginia and North Carolina. We originally called it "Sex in the Cornfields," but we've since adopted a more decorous title, "Whoopee in the Cornfields."

My directors and I often tell people that networking is more about farming than it is about hunting. Once, when Art was expounding on this theme, someone in the audience raised his hand and asked, "Do you honestly believe that?"

Art said, "Of course. It's about cultivating relationships."

"So you're telling me that we could actually learn something about networking from a farmer?"

"Well, no, not literally," said Art. "We're talking figuratively. We're saying it's *like* farming. Why do you ask?"

This is an organization where anybody here will help you with your business. It's that kind of sharing from the top down. They want to see everybody else succeed. There's no information ownership — you know, if I'm going to look good, you'll have to look bad.

— Emory Cowan
Co-Executive Director
BNI Colorado

"Well, I'll tell you. I read a story about a farmer in Nebraska who had won the state fair four times in a row with his corn. Nobody had ever done that before, so the paper sent someone out to interview him.

"The reporter asked, 'What is your secret? Do you use a special corn seed?'

"The farmer said, 'Absolutely. I develop my own corn seed, and that's an important aspect of it.'

"'Well, then, that's your secret,' said the reporter. 'You plant a type of corn that's different from that of your neighbors.'

"'No, I also give it to my neighbors,' said the farmer.

"'You give it to your neighbors?' asked the incredulous reporter. 'Why in the world would you give your award-winning corn to your neighbors?'

"The farmer said, 'Well, you've got to understand how corn is pollinated. It's pollinated from neighboring fields. And if you've got fields around you that don't have this top-quality corn, your field is not going to grow top-quality corn either. But if my neighbor's field has this really strong corn, I have awesome corn. And that's how I've won at the Nebraska State Fair the last four years in a row.'"

I like this story because it's a great metaphor for how this organization works. Why join BNI? So you can help other people and be helped in return.

While we're on the subject, why is networking more about farming than about hunting?

Marketing is sometimes approached as a sort of big-game hunt. The customers are out there in the woods; you have to load up with your best ads and promotional materials and seek them out, one by one. If you're a good shot, you get instant satisfaction. The more you bag, the better your business — but it's hard work, and you can never rest. You have to go out every day and find more big game.

Building a business through referral networking is more like farming. Unlike hunting, you don't expect instant returns. Instead, you cultivate relationships by offering others referrals, expert assistance, and other benefits. You form long-lasting referral partnerships based on trust. And if you are steadfast and patient, your efforts will pay off and you will reap a bountiful harvest: business opportunities that your networking partners refer to you.

The stories I told you about San Francisco and Montana are good illustrations of this principle on the organizational scale. When the idea popped into my head that the Bay Area was the next logical BNI region, I jumped on a plane and flew there, armed to the teeth with brochures, hunting for strangers I might persuade to start and run BNI in a high-potential region. It was like traveling to a totally unknown area to hunt because, well, there's got to be something there, right?

But while I had my sights focused on scaring a new Regional Director out of the brush, my garden back home was growing and starting to produce. In fact, it was spreading all over the place. All I had to do was help the directors I already had sow the idea in new plots, transplant some of the fast-growing shoots into fertile soil, and let the crop grow naturally. Soon, the harvest from those fields would be almost more than I could handle.

TRAINING AND EDUCATION

One of the most important BNI traditions is our commitment to training and education in following a system that's based on experience. This tradition is one of BNI's core competencies.

For the first year of BNI's existence, we didn't have anything that could be called Leadership Team training. When we started training in the second year, our first Leadership Team manual consisted of only two pages — the Agenda. Today my directors, staff, and I conduct over 100,000 person-hours of training each year, guided by a 500-page manual. That's a lot of training and a lot of details, but it's part of what has made BNI a lasting and growing success.

Another key factor in our success is our early adoption of the Certified Networker Program and our strong focus on member education. We have numerous trainers who have collectively trained thousands of BNI members on various networking topics to increase their success. Needless to say, we have some amazing BNI members and chapters as a result.

— David Alexander
Executive Director
BNI Georgia

Why does training work? It preserves the system and the culture; it keeps us from making the same errors again and again. Over the years of starting new chapters, new regions, and new countries, we've made every mistake you can think of (and a whole bunch that you'd never think of), and we've learned from them. We know how to avoid the mistakes, how to run the organization right. Training is how we pass along this wisdom to leaders and members so they can avoid having to learn the hard way.

Training the directors, who then train their Leadership Teams, is the top link in BNI's chain of training. Today almost all of our director training is conducted by four experienced BNI Executive Directors: Margie and Emory Cowan of Colorado, Art Radtke of Virginia, and David Alexander of Georgia.

KEEPING THE FUN IN THE FUNDAMENTALS

If you're not enjoying the journey, you're probably not going to enjoy the destination. That seems self-evident, but it didn't become clear to me right away. Having realized early the importance of training, we had placed most of our emphasis there for many years and had somewhat lost sight of one of BNI's early charms — the fact that everybody enjoyed and looked forward to going to the meetings. Sometime around 1988 I figured out that it's possible to stay focused on your objectives and still have fun.

There are a lot of different ways to have fun at a meeting and yet stick to the structure. Meeting Stimulants are one of the ways BNI does it. We have several dozen different kinds of Meeting Stimulants, so chapters can find lots of different ways to liven up their meetings without repeating themselves. (See your BNI director for a copy of *Meeting Stimulants.*)

In one versatile Meeting Stimulant, you put your business card into a basket. The basket is passed around the room, and you draw a card. You then give a 60-second presentation for the person whose card you drew. It's a real learning experience. How well do you know the other person's business? How well have you communicated your own business to the person who drew your card?

It's also an opportunity to get creative and have a lot of fun. Many people do an impression of the other person, using the same speaking style and gestures. One woman who was very short drew the card of the tallest person in the chapter. She pulled out her chair and stood on it to give his presentation.

Another big hit is something we call the "BNI Radio Show." The chapter President plays the part of a disk jockey running a radio music show that consists mostly of 60-second commercial breaks — and 60 seconds means 60 seconds. If you give a 50-second presentation, you get 10 seconds of dead air — you're left standing there in total silence with everybody looking at you. If you run long, you're cut off in mid-sentence. Knowing you're responsible for exactly 60 seconds of "air time" gives you great incentive to polish your presentation.

I've seen some truly awesome "Radio Show" presentations. One member, the owner of John's Auto Body, did a "man on the street" interview. He walked around with a microphone and asked members, "Would you like to tell us about your experience with John's Auto Body?" He got a lot of interesting responses.

When they know they're going to have to perform, people actually prepare. Some can just stand up and wing it, but most give a lot of thought to what they're going to say. In a meeting that's enlivened by a Meeting Stimulant, members may learn more about fellow members in an hour than they've learned before in five hours of meetings. Some Meeting Stimulants may seem silly, but members have fun, and most important, they focus on doing business.

Having fun with the fundamentals means more than just members entertaining members with their presentations. It means maintaining, in a positive way, the integrity of the process. It means positive accountability.

Every organization has to maintain order and discipline. I have often said that controlling the behavior of an organization made up almost entirely of independent business people is like herding cats. It takes patience and grit to keep things going in the right direction, but it must not involve discipline applied for its own sake.

The way BNI handles the cell phone problem — and everybody knows what I mean by that — is a good illustration of how order and decorum can be preserved by maintaining an atmosphere of positive accountability.

A few years back, I was speaking to a large gathering of members at a big BNI event hosted by Executive Director Dan Georgevich in Michigan. In the middle of my talk, someone's cell phone began ringing. Suddenly, 400 people were singing "Happy Birthday" at the top of their voices!

I stood there like a deer in the headlights. I knew it wasn't my birthday. Whose was it, and what was so urgent about it?

Dan ran up to me and said, "I'm sorry, I'm sorry. I've trained them to sing 'Happy Birthday' whenever someone's cell phone goes off in a meeting."

I laughed. "What a great idea!"

"Well, it usually works," said Dan. "At least, when I remember to tell new members and visitors."

BNI is a relationship business. We're farmers. We cultivate each other, we feed each other. The worst members are the hunters, the ones who want to take constantly. They come in and think, I'm sitting here and nobody's passing me business. This doesn't work. I generally don't encourage those people to stay.

— Gayle Williams
Executive Director
BNI New Mexico

It's a terrific example of positive accountability. It works, because nobody wants to become the center of attention because of a rude cell phone. But when it happens, at least everybody gets a good laugh — even the miscreant, once the embarrassment passes.

Here's another example of positive accountability and keeping the fun in the fundamentals. At one of our San Fernando Valley chapters, a newly elected President confronted the members with a problem. "We were a great chapter a year ago, but we've been backsliding. Today I'd like to get everybody's commitment that we're going to get back to the basics. We're going to follow the system and do it well. Are we all okay with that?" Everybody agreed. They would make a major effort to abide by the rules.

One of their biggest problems was attendance. Sure enough, only three weeks into their reform effort, one member missed his third meeting of the year.

The standard response would have been for the Membership Committee to send a "nastygram," a letter to the member stating that another absence could force the Membership Committee to open his classification. The chapter President felt that this was unduly harsh. Instead, he got creative.

At the end of the chapter meeting, he said, "I need all of you to do me a personal favor. It's not hard, and it will only take a minute."

Several people said they would help him out.

"No, no, I need all of you. I need your full commitment. Look, I'll tell you what it is, and if you think it's too hard, you can say so. I promise you, it's not hard, but I need everybody's commitment." Slowly, more hands went up, and finally all 23 members there were on board.

"Great!" said the President. "Now, here's what I want you to do. John missed the meeting again today. He's missed three of the last five meetings. Remember how we talked about getting back to the basics, three weeks ago? Now, John's a good member, and we don't want to lose him, but he's apparently lost sight of how important it is to come to every meeting.

"So, rather than send him the letter, let's all give him a call. And I don't mean wait a few days and call him. I mean call him right now. As soon as you leave the meeting, pick up your cell phone or find a pay phone and give him a call, or call him the minute you get to your office. Everybody needs to give him a call within the next two hours. Will you do that?"

They laughed. Yes, they would. And they did exactly that.

Now, I happened to be at the following week's meeting, and John showed up. He was laughing. "What the hell did you guys do last week? I come into the office, and my receptionist is going, 'John, the phone is ringing off the hook, it's all these people from BNI.' So I start answering the phone, and we get 18 telephone calls before 10:00 in the morning.

"Hey, I get it! I won't miss any more meetings! I'll be here! You guys are all crazy!"

He wasn't the only one who got it. All 23 members who called him got it, too. Nobody got mad. They all had a good laugh — but the message stuck. Attendance improved.

One of the strengths of BNI is that we're all friends — and it's also one of the weaknesses. We like and trust each other, and we don't like to find ourselves in the position of having to hold a friend accountable. This reluctance can turn a disciplined networking organization into a coffee klatch. Positive accountability makes it easier to maintain discipline without alienating friends.

TESTIMONIALS

One of our oldest traditions came from an early change in our Agenda: testimonials (see chapter 3). Barely two months into BNI's first year, we decided that if you didn't have any referrals to pass along at the weekly meeting, you could give a testimonial instead. You could talk about another member's business, product, or service, or even about the individual herself, speaking from the heart and being very specific. This was a positive way of giving support to another member in lieu of an actual referral. It was quite valuable, not only in giving the individual moral support but in bringing other members' attention, and quite possibly referrals, to the individual's products or services.

But what if — and this is a pretty big "if," considering how many options you have — you arrive at a meeting unprepared to give a testimonial, and you don't have a referral? Well, over the years, we've increased your options even more. We've redefined the Agenda item. We no longer define it as simply passing referrals, which to some members implies that not having a referral to pass at a given meeting equates to failure. We now ask simply that you think of this Agenda item as your opportunity to make an "I have" statement.

What's an "I have" statement? It's a specific, positive statement to or about a member, your BNI chapter, or BNI as an organization. It can be "I have a referral for Jane." It can be "I have a story to tell you about a great experience I had doing business with Jack." Or it can be "I have something to say about what being in this organization has meant to me" — such as the camaraderie of the group, opportunities to develop lifelong friendships, access to information and ideas.

Making an "I have" statement helps improve your networking relationships and strengthens the group. Even if you haven't given or gotten a lot of business, there's something positive about this process, especially for visitors who are considering becoming members.

CARING ABOUT PEOPLE

This is a tradition that members may not be directly aware of but that is carried forward by our directors. Here is how this tradition is stated in full:

People don't care how much you know unless they know how much you care.

Our directors are the best in the world in knowing how to run a networking organization. But this doesn't matter unless members understand how much their directors care about them. One of the first things I tell directors is not to be a "seagull director" — someone who flies in, makes a lot of noise, dumps on everyone, then flies out. Directors have to be out in the field as much as possible, among the members, helping the Leadership Team, solving problems, helping where needed.

The director needs to be known and trusted. This is a philosophy that members should probably be taught as well. It sets a high and positive standard to follow when dealing with other members, as well as with customers, colleagues, employees, and vendors. You can be the best at whatever business you're in, but unless the other members know that you care about them, they're not going to care about how much you know. That will affect all your relationships, both business and personal.

I often urge people to memorize and use five magic words that can go a long way toward solving any problem: "How can I help you?" These five words are an excellent way to start the process of showing people that you care, especially when used by the Leadership and Membership Teams of a chapter. Rather than confronting a member and saying, "You're not bringing any referrals into the chapter — you need to do better," the approach should be "How can I help you bring more referrals to the meeting?"

Using the five magic words fits the BNI philosophy of Givers Gain. It goes a long way toward finding a mutually agreeable solution to a problem — and does wonders for everyone's blood pressure.

WALKING THE TALK

One critical element of being successful in referral networking is practicing what you preach. All of us — members, staff, Leadership Teams, directors — represent BNI to everyone we meet; it's important that we walk the talk.

We teach that it is important to bring in referrals; therefore, every one of us should bring in referrals. We know that it is important to bring in visitors, so we should all bring in visitors. If we say that it's important to build trusting relationships, we should be the first people out there doing that. And the more you give — the more you walk the talk — the more you receive.

I see this every day: the most successful chapters, the most successful members, the most successful directors — they all walk the talk. There is no disparity between what they say and what they do. Always remember:

> **"What you do thunders so loudly above your head that I cannot hear the words you speak."**

YOUR INVESTMENT

Membership in BNI is not a guarantee; it is an opportunity to turn your time and commitment into a lot of money. The question is, What are you going to create with the opportunity that you have?

There's an old business truism that's useful here. Think of your investment in BNI as a bar of iron. A plain bar of iron is worth about $5. But if you turn it into horseshoes (I *said* it was old), it's worth $10.

If you turn it into screwdrivers, it's worth $250.

If you turn it into needles, it's worth $3,500.

If you turn it into balance springs for watches, it's worth $250,000.

You have a membership in this organization, and turning that into value involves understanding the traditions of this organization.

It involves Givers Gain — giving to other people in order to get business from other people.

It involves going to every single education and training opportunity that we can offer you.

It involves keeping the fun in the fundamentals; you've got to have fun while you're doing this.

It involves learning how to do effective testimonials.

It involves showing people that you truly care about their success.

And it involves walking the talk.

These are the traditions that have made BNI the world's most successful referral networking organization.

THE SECRET TO SUCCESS

That's about all the preaching I'm going to do in this book. If I have any sermons left in me, I'll do what I usually do: take them home and use them on my kids.

Visitors to my home will tell you that I often call on my young son, Trey, for support when I'm trying to make a point. He's pretty familiar with my arguments, so he can usually be relied on to take my side.

But I've started to think that maybe I've leaned on him a little too much. The other day I asked him to tell a visitor the secret to achieving success without hard work.

"The secret of success without hard work is still a secret," said Trey, a bit wearily. "Now can I go out and play?"

Trey's right, of course. Hard work is essential. But so is vision, and that's what my last chapter is about.

chapter 11

20/20 VISION
2005–????

BECAUSE BNI WAS ABOUT TO OPEN ITS 20TH COUNTRY, THE FOUNDER'S CIRCLE decided that "20/20 Vision: 20 Years, 20 Countries" should be the organization's theme for BNI's 20th anniversary in 2005.

It is a fitting theme that resonates with me in many ways. However, it implies that I had a clear vision of what this organization would become when I started it in 1985 as a 28-year-old business consultant — and that would be an overstatement, at least. It took time for my vision for BNI to come into focus.

I spent my early years in BNI, with the help of members and directors, devising a referral networking system that would work well and keep on working. Creating a truly effective system took time — and it is a never-ending task, because we must keep improving if we wish to remain the best.

Not until that system was substantially in place did the vision truly start to come into focus. It began with my recognition that, like me, many business owners were looking for a focused, organized, positive, and supportive networking program that could increase their business through referrals. Before long I realized that this concept struck a chord with a much larger audience than I had imagined.

In the late '80s I began to think BNI could be an international organization. It took several more years to create the corporate infrastructure necessary to make that happen. The early '90s were spent spreading the program across the United States. However, our real triumph came in the mid-'90s, when my vision of an international organization

became a reality. From that point on, BNI's growth has been truly phenomenal. Now we routinely open as many chapters in one year as we
did in our first 10 years combined.

A Moment in Time

Where are we now? It's hard to take a good snapshot of BNI; we're so
large, and moving so fast, that the picture comes out blurred. But here's a
quick look at BNI worldwide on the occasion of our 20th anniversary:

Number of members	**72,000**
Number of chapters	**3,600**
Number of directors	**600**
Number of countries	**20**
Number of continents	**5**

Pretty impressive, isn't it? A graph showing how the number of chapters has grown is rather amazing, too. We're adding about a chapter a
day now, somewhere in the world.

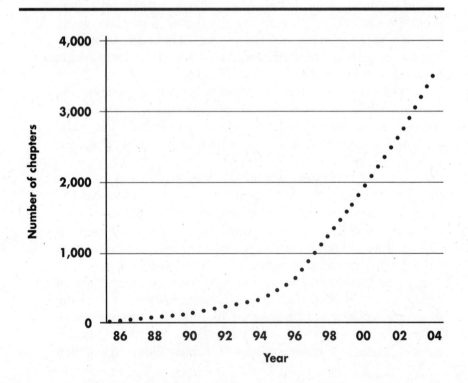

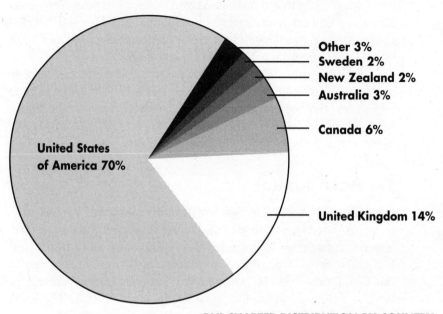

Other 3%
Sweden 2%
New Zealand 2%
Australia 3%

Canada 6%

United States
of America 70%

United Kingdom 14%

BNI CHAPTER DISTRIBUTION BY COUNTRY

This phenomenal growth, which was not even dented by the two recessions that it spanned, is testament not only to the vitality of BNI's central vision but to the quality, commitment, creativity, generosity, and loyalty of its leaders and members. Every time I visit a chapter, anywhere in the world, I am pleased and amazed to see how thoroughly the BNI philosophy, Givers Gain, has shaped its activity at every level, and how selfless BNI members are toward their fellow members and their communities. There's a saying that I like: "You may not make a world of difference, but you can make a difference in the world." I think that BNI makes a difference in the world by helping business people succeed, and I am proud to be a small part of that.

But that's history. It's the future that's important now. It is for the future that I, along with the considerable assistance of Jeff Morris (my longtime editor and friend), wrote this book.

Among all the organizations I have seen, BNI is unique: it has an organizational philosophy that is inculcated throughout the organization, from top to bottom. With Givers Gain as the foundation, a powerful organizational culture has evolved — one that is based on directors, members, and BNI staff giving their time and assistance to one another so that everyone might succeed more effectively in their business. New directors and members who come to our National and International BNI Conferences often tell me, "I have never seen anything like this. Everyone is here to freely give advice and help others."

In order for us to maintain that culture — or better yet, nurture and continue to build upon that culture — I believe it is important to understand our beginnings as well as to create a vision for the future. Most of this book has been about how the company has evolved. I would like to end it with my vision for what lies ahead.

THE ROAD AHEAD

What do we expect BNI to look like in another 10 years? We will grow faster in other countries than in the United States, simply because there is so much virgin territory around the world where BNI can take root. Right now, about 70 percent of our chapters are in the US, 30 percent in other countries. Based on how well BNI has been received around the world, I feel it's inevitable that someday the organization will be larger outside the US. That 70/30 will almost certainly become 30/70.

The growth in the number of chapters shows no signs of slowing down. By the end of the decade, I believe we will have more than 5,000 chapters worldwide. To handle the international growth we have already experienced, as well as what is to come, we've already revamped our Franchise Advisory Board and renamed it the International Franchise Advisory Board. This evolution has improved accountability among franchises in the field, heading off business conflicts before they can rise to the level of problems that would have to be solved at BNI headquarters. Although members are not aware of most of the Franchise Advisory Board's activities, this body is instrumental in keeping the business end of BNI running smoothly. When the board is doing its job well, the chapters work better and members are better served.

All individuals are created absolutely equal in the eyes of BNI. You have equal access to the results that anyone else could get through the relationships you commit to invest in, whether you're a brand-new member selling vitamins or a banker who's been there a long time.

—Stacia Robinson
Executive Director
BNI Alabama

Another aspect of BNI's tremendous growth, both in the United States and around the world, is the rising number of cultures the organization must recognize and represent. To help us understand our differences better and to increase the number of representative business owners of diverse cultures in BNI chapters, we've established a Cross-Cultural Council, a volunteer group of BNI directors and members. Headed by its founding Chair, Executive Director Stacia Robinson of Montgomery, Alabama, the council develops cross-cultural policies and guidelines and educates and trains staff, directors, and members about cross-cultural issues. It meets at Directors' Conferences and communicates by e-mail and periodic teleconferences.

Although our international growth will most likely outpace growth in the US, our studies show there is tremendous potential for growth there as well. New chapters that are formed in these areas have no trouble finding eager new members who quickly go to work generating high-quality referrals. We are far from the saturation point.

As we fill in the gaps between existing chapters, however, we've become aware that our old chapter naming system isn't up to snuff. If you open the first chapter in Springfield and call yourself the Springfield Chapter, you're being unfair to the other 25 chapters that may start up in the general area. But if you are the BNI Business Builders of Springfield, then the next chapter, which meets 10 blocks down the street from you, can call itself the BNI Referral Kings, and everybody's happy.

Other studies we've done indicate that in the developed nations, such as the United States, Canada, United Kingdom, Australia, New Zealand, Sweden, and Germany, we should be able to open one chapter for every 25,000 to 30,000 people, or somewhere between 33 and 40 chapters for every million in population.

That's an enormous number — something like 10,000 chapters in the United States alone, three times as many as we have worldwide right now. I believe we will have more than 15,000 chapters worldwide within the foreseeable future. How's that for growth potential?

EDUCATION

Networking is one of the best ways to build a business, yet we don't teach it in colleges or universities around the world. We give people business degrees, but we teach them hardly anything about the one subject that virtually all business people say is critically important to their business: networking.

Although BNI is not an educational institution, education is a cornerstone of its success. We have spent several decades developing and codifying a body of knowledge and material that is second to no other organization in the world. Today, BNI has thousands of pages of support material to help any business person in the world who is willing to take the time to study the concepts and, most important, practice the procedures BNI has developed.

It's worth repeating: no other networking organization anywhere in the world devotes as much time and energy to teaching people how to build their business through word of mouth. Training is one of the core competencies that BNI must continue to emphasize.

Opportunity has been known to knock, but it doesn't turn the knob and walk through the door for anyone. That part is up to you. As a member, you should expect your Leadership Team to be well trained and your director to provide value-added information with each visit. You should also take advantage of the wealth of information available through your online newsletter, SuccessNet, as well as national and international websites such as www.bni.com.

You are part of an organization that offers a wealth of networking-related support material and assistance second to no other referral organization in the world. To ensure that BNI remains the world leader, we will continue to enhance our support materials, Meeting Stimulants, and manuals, and to introduce other creative programs, such as the Reciprocity Ring, a networking tool designed to enhance the sharing of referrals.

Strategic Alliances

As we continue to become a global force, strategic alliances with select organizations will help us to achieve that. I believe that BNI will continue to build strong relationships with key companies and organizations around the world. I believe we will continue to develop strategic alliances with companies that have a symbiotic relationship with the organization. Some of our early alliances have involved the Royal Bank of Scotland, Brian Buffini Seminars, Coffee News, Brian Tracy International, the Referral Institute, and Jim Blasingame's radio show, "The Small Business Advocate." Each of these organizations has in some way helped us design a process that will continue to spread BNI's name throughout the business community worldwide.

We also have strategic alliances with many authors and speakers who spread the word about networking and word-of-mouth marketing.

People like Susan RoAne, Bob Burg, Robyn Henderson, Ron Sukenick, Robert Davis, and many more are important to the organization because they act as unofficial ambassadors for networking and have helped make the BNI name an international brand. Today, most books on networking either discuss BNI at length or at least mention it. To keep our name in the marketplace, we will continue to maintain and enhance BNI's relationship with popular authors.

INTEGRATING TECHNOLOGY

BNI is already invested in new technologies that will help us grow and develop to our full potential. One example I've already mentioned is our new database system. BNINET enables us to accurately measure our key success factors, such as the number of chapters in a region, average membership per chapter, retention, and — in the future — market penetration. This will help us keep tabs on our rapid growth and will revolutionize the way we manage our operations worldwide.

Strategic alliances with companies like ZeroDegrees.com and Knowmentum.com will keep us on the cutting edge of rapidly developing trends such as social networking technology, which support the kind of in-person networking that BNI is all about. Online communities such as Coachville's "Networking & Social Capital" website and Yahoo's "BNIOfficialGroup" chat room provide a forum for BNI members and nonmembers to talk about networking, word-of-mouth marketing, and social capital. They flatten the communication hierarchy and let members, directors, and other interested parties communicate with one another from anywhere in the world.

CREATIVE MARKETING

BNI is a word-of-mouth–based organization. We've built this company through word of mouth, and I believe that's the best way to continue to build it.

In local terms, the best way to build a chapter is for one person to ask another person to a meeting. In global terms, however, it's about spreading the brand through books and articles about the organization — that is, word of mouth on a larger scale.

To keep our name and worldwide brand in the business community's radar, we will continue to publish books and magazine articles regularly. Our fingerprints are all over these materials. When people read our books, they not only learn many examples of how word of mouth works, they see occasional references to BNI.

I learned many years ago that the media don't want to interview you about your business. Want to be in the paper? "Take out an ad." But they'll interview any idiot with a book — and I have lots of books. This strategy has worked well for us. In our first 10 years, BNI opened more than 300 chapters. Over the next 10 years, with books and articles spreading the word internationally, we opened more than 3,000 chapters!

VISION

You are part of a remarkable organization — an organization whose primary purpose is to help you increase your business through referrals. I've often said that in a local chapter you see only the tip of the iceberg. I hope that this book has given you a glimpse of what lies beneath the surface. This organization rests on an incredibly strong foundation that is made up of some of the hardest-working and most dedicated people I have ever met. I have seen amazing commitment at all levels, from the BNI staff to directors, Leadership Teams, and members. You are part of something bigger than what you see from week to week, and it is my hope that the stories and traditions discussed in this book help you to see that.

If all the people in an organization row in the same direction, that organization can dominate any industry, in any market, against any competition, at any time. BNI has dominated its industry in almost every market, against all the competition, for almost a decade now. It has happened because of a *shared vision* and a *shared implementation of that vision.*

I invite you to share the vision and be part of Givers Gain.

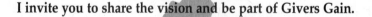

INDEX

6

BNI CODE OF ETHICS

Upon acceptance to BNI, I agree to abide by the following Code of Ethics during the service of my participation in the organization:

1. I will provide the quality of services at the prices that I have quoted.

2. I will be truthful with the members and their referrals.

3. I will build goodwill and trust among members and their referrals.

4. I will take responsibility for following up on the referrals I receive.

5. I will display a positive and supportive attitude with BNI members.

6. I will live up to the ethical standards of my profession.

(Note: Professional standards outlined in a formal code of ethics supersede the above standards.)

Member Launching Pad

BNI is all about education. You educate your fellow chapter members about what you do and what is a good referral for you. Likewise, the other members of your chapter educate you in the same manner. This education takes place in four ways: (1) your 60-second commercial, (2) your 10-minute presentation, (3) the 15 minutes of open networking before the Agenda begins, and (4) One-on-One Dance Cards with other members.

It is important for you to be prepared so that you can utilize these educational opportunities to your greatest advantage. Spend some time identifying the following:

Launching Pad Questions

My 3 best customers are:

1. _____
2. _____
3. _____

Examples of referrals that work well for me are:

1. _____
2. _____
3. _____

My best Contact Sphere professions are:

1. _____
2. _____
3. _____

New doors I'd like to open are:

1. _____
2. _____
3. _____

ONE-ON-ONE DANCE CARD

An opportunity to get to know your chapter members and their businesses better.

	Date/Time	Partners	Location
Week 1			
Week 2			
Week 3			
Week 4			
Week 5			
Week 6			
Week 7			
Week 8			
Week 9			
Week 10			

By meeting repeatedly with all other members, you will increase your rapport with members. Increased rapport leads to more opportunity to give and receive referrals.

About BNI

BNI (Business Network Int'l.) was founded by Dr. Ivan Misner in 1985 as a way for business people to generate referrals in a structured, professional environment. The organization, now the world's largest referral network, has tens of thousands of members on almost every continent of the world. Since its inception, members of BNI have passed millions of referrals, generating billions of dollars for the participants.

The primary purpose of the organization is to pass qualified business referrals to the members. The philosophy of BNI may be summed up in two simple words: "Givers Gain." If you give business to people, you will get business from them. BNI allows only one person per profession to join a chapter. The program is designed for business people to develop long-term relationships, thereby creating a basis for trust and, inevitably, referrals. The mission of BNI is to help members increase their business through a structured, positive, and professional "word-of-mouth" program that enables them to develop long-term, meaningful relationships with quality business professionals.

To visit a chapter near you, contact BNI on the Internet at www.bni.com for international information and www.bni.canada.ca for Canadian information.